PSYCHIC
DREAMWALKING

PSYCHIC DREAMWALKING

explorations at the edge of self

MICHELLE BELANGER

WEISER BOOKS
San Francisco, CA / Newburyport, MA

First published in 2006 by
Red Wheel/Weiser, LLC
With offices at:
500 Third Street, Suite 230
San Francisco, CA 94107

ISBN-13: 978-1-57863-386-9

Cover and interior design by MAIJA TOLLEFSON
Typeset in Electra and Alita
Cover photograph © 2006 by CHRISTOPHER ROSSI

Printed in the U.S.A.

CONTENTS

THE AUTHOR WOULD LIKE TO GRATEFULLY THANK DAN, DAWN, AND THE CIRCLE OF THE SACRED FLAME FOR THEIR HELPFUL INPUT ON THIS BOOK; JOSH, KWEI, AND MY OTHER DREAMING PARTNERS; AND ALSO CHARLIE AND CONNIE FOR PROVIDING A QUIET PLACE TO WRITE DURING THE VIDEO SHOOT.

THIS BOOK IS DEDICATED TO NEIL GAIMAN, THE MAN WHO GAVE A FACE TO DREAM.

PRAYER OF THE DREAMING

I commit myself to you, Lord Morpheus!
Open wide the Gates of Dream.
Grant me safe passage in your realm
So I may return with tales to tell.

A LITTLE GIRL'S DREAM

I FIRST ENCOUNTERED THE CONCEPT OF DREAMWALKING in the fourth grade. It was 1982. Ronald Reagan had been in office for only a year. When one of my math problems came out to 444, all I could think about were the sixty-six hostages who had been held in Iran for exactly that number of days. Troubles with Iran's neighbor, Iraq, were a dim cloud on a distant horizon.

If that seems like an early age to begin studying the occult, consider that this was also the era of such TV shows as *That's Incredible!*, *In Search Of*, and *Ripley's Believe It or Not*. I had practically been weaned on my family's tales of their psychic experiences and vivid encounters with ghosts, although such tales were never recounted in mixed company.

The weird and the occult seemed part of the very fabric of my early childhood. The sleepy Ohio town in which I grew up boasted its own haunted library, and I had personally met the main ghost, a winsome lady in a blue-patterned dress, before I was in kindergarten. Add to this the fact that I'd had at least two NDEs (near-death experiences) and two OBEs (out-of-body experiences) by the tender age of five, and it's no wonder that my life led me not only to study but also to write about occult topics.

Fourth grade was a significant year for several reasons. First, it was the year that I was placed in my school district's "gifted" program. Second, a direct consequence of the first, it was the year that I got switched from Hinckley Elementary to the Sharon school district, a thirty-minute bus ride away. It was also the year that I started seriously reading up on metaphysics and the occult, thanks in part to a more extensive library that included a much-thumbed tome with colorful articles on the human aura, ghosts, UFOs, and astral projection.

It was also the year I met Pearl Cantley.

Pearl is something of an enigma to me even now. I'm well aware of that old magickal adage, "When the student is ready, the teacher will come," but never in a million years would I have expected to find such an unlikely mentor. Pearl was, to say the least, a strange child. Undersized and sickly, she wore thick pop-bottle glasses that made her watery green eyes look insectoid, as if she was an alien participating in some weird school-exchange program. Adding to the sense that there was something not only different but perhaps wholly alien about Pearl was the fact that she was virtually an albino. There was a washed-out quality to the color of her skin, hair, and eyes that made this tiny, fey fourth-grader seem like a faded projection glimmering dimly in a world of full color.

Pearl was socially quirky, if not full-out eccentric, paying attention to people only when it suited her and more often than not wrapped entirely in her own internal world. That Pearl was probably a high-functioning autistic seems likely from the vantage point of memory. All I knew at the time was that she was my polar opposite academically: where I got taken out of normal classes to design spaceships and contemplate the beginnings of algebra with the other gifted students, Pearl was in the "special" classes, often vexing her teachers with that stubborn refusal to even acknowledge their existence, happier to remain wandering the fields of her mind.

There are times when I have seriously wondered whether Pearl wasn't some being conjured up by my own imagination. For the sake of my own sanity, I've gone back through old school pictures and even called up the school district to make certain that Pearl did indeed exist. Some of my experiences with her, if they happened exactly as I recall, were unusual enough to give a little credence to the alien theory, although I believe that in modern magickal lingo, Pearl would more likely be termed "Otherkin." Other ideas that have presented themselves are that Pearl was a walk-in or perhaps a simple but very open individual who, unbeknownst to her, channeled some higher entity. And of course, I've never overlooked the possibility that Pearl could have simply been insane—albeit a lunatic whose delusions often had an observable impact on the outside world.

Whatever the reason for it, Pearl was different. And for some reason, she gravitated straight to me, the new kid who, admittedly, was just as introverted and socially awkward as herself. Pearl's first words to me were a foretaste of her usual blunt and yet mysterious manner of speaking:

"I've been sent to teach you."

To an inquisitive fourth-grader, this was an irresistible invitation to adventure. When you're that age, you want to believe that the world is far more mysterious than your parents and teachers allow it to be, and you're just naïve enough to believe that you can take on all of its challenges without any difficulty. I didn't question what Pearl was supposed to teach me or even who could have possibly "sent" her to me. After all, it was just coincidence that we found ourselves in the same school, in the same class, and sitting next to one another . . . right?

Her words implied that we were part of something bigger than ourselves, that there was a purpose and a plan for each of us in the universe. That sense of something bigger, along with the sheer mystery of the project, would keep me glued to her, even in those times when her words made no sense to me at all and I was gripped with the sneaking suspicion that she was not a visionary but simply insane.

CHILD'S PLAY

Although I was intrigued by her, Pearl did not have a wholly willing student in me. I have never been the most trusting of people, and I have always had a mile-wide skeptical streak, especially when it comes to supposed "authorities." My great-aunt was a social worker, and throughout my childhood, she taught me a great deal about psychology. I knew the term "schizophrenic" by the time I met Pearl, and while I did not have an advanced comprehension of that disorder, I understood enough to suspect that Pearl's beliefs might simply be symptoms of that disease.

Thoughts of schizophrenia were constantly in the back of my mind when I interacted with Pearl, making me always of two minds when we "played." On one hand, I was fascinated by the psychic techniques she imparted to me, but on the other, I doubted everything. There was always the nagging suspicion that she might be crazy, and I worried that believing her might make me crazy, too. I had no trouble learning the principles of a technique, but I never really believed in it until I had tested it over and over again on my own, getting the same results each time. Even then, stubborn as I was, I would still wonder whether or not the results were a product of wishful thinking. Thanks to my highly educated great-aunt, the word "psychosomatic" was familiar to me as well.

The day that Pearl surpassed my ability to doubt her—at least on some level—was the day she taught me shielding. This was a rather spontaneous lesson, brought about by those cruel games children play with those they feel are different from them.

We were in the schoolyard at recess, and some of the older kids had been playing dodgeball. Recess was almost over, so it was time for them to put the balls away. I'm not quite certain what Pearl did to earn their wrath. In truth, she got picked on a lot simply because she didn't fit in and showed no interest in ever wanting to. Certainly, her lack of social skills did not help the situation.

The fifth-graders, carrying those big red rubber balls that were standard issue to schools of the day, walked toward us. One of them called something out to Pearl, and she ignored him. A few more catcalls ensued, with Pearl continuing to just stare at them as they approached. I can't say I was any better. Just a few steps behind her, I wanted to leave, but since Pearl hadn't budged, I stood around waiting to see what would happen next. Not that it took a genius to guess exactly what that would be.

However, just before the balls started to fly, Pearl turned her head slightly in my direction and, without losing that faraway gaze, said, "Don't move. Watch me."

And then she closed her eyes and bowed her head a little. I could see her hands balled into little fists at her sides, and she began humming tunelessly, the same note over and over again, just loud enough for me to hear. It sounded just like the testing note that played on the TV when all the programs were over and the screen faded to snow.

The first ball sailed through the air, aimed squarely at Pearl's head. But when it got within two feet of her, it veered off suddenly. It struck the pavement about five feet to her left, then bounced away harmlessly into the grass. The second ball came at her, aimed decisively at her midsection. The girl who threw this one was already recognized as one of the jocks at the school. She had power and accuracy behind that throw, and yet this ball, too, veered off suddenly and bounced away.

At this point, it became a challenge for the other kids to try to hit Pearl with the balls. A few students in the knot of players still had balls tucked under their arms, and these were aimed with many exaggerated gestures and oaths that *this* one *this* time would strike "the freak." The other balls were collected from the pavement and the grass, and new tormentors took aim.

Throughout all of this, Pearl just stood there, body taut, fists clenched, humming that single, ear-scratching tone. She never flinched, and as far as I could tell, she never opened her eyes.

Balls continued to fly. One of them sailed over her head and nearly hit me. I sidestepped it, clumsily, most of my attention on the spectacle unfolding with Pearl.

Nothing hit her. Certainly some of the balls were badly aimed, but she was a stationary target, and these were regular dodgeball players. The other kids were shouting, making boasts, carrying on eagerly to see which of them could knock her glasses off her face from ten paces away. And despite their enthusiasm, despite everything, Pearl remained untouched. Balls would seemingly defy the laws of physics to avoid her. One astounding ball appeared to strike something a foot in front of Pearl's face. It bounced off of this invisible barrier as surely as if encountering a brick wall.

And Pearl just kept standing there, humming with her eyes closed.

Although this seemed to drag on forever, it probably only lasted about five minutes. The recess monitors were as vigilant as Argus, and two of them came hurrying over, yelling at the dodgeball players to cease and desist. Students scattered, but Pearl remained fixed. The only difference was that now her eyes were open, and she was staring at her tormentors with that vaguely unfocused, watery gaze filtered through half an inch of distorting lens.

As was normally the case, the recess monitors grabbed whoever was too slow to run away, which included both Pearl and myself. We all got yelled at, regardless of who did or did not start anything, and received stern admonishments to play together nicely.

Standing in line, waiting to go back into the building, I was still replaying the incident in my head, trying to come up with some logical reason for what I had seen. The wind was not particularly strong that day, and the balls had not all followed the same trajectory when veering away. Certainly, the students could have simply missed, but missing again and again, especially when these were youngsters who were skilled at sports . . . well, it wasn't adding up in my head. Pearl did not help my quest for denial when she approached me in class later that day and asked, "Do you want to learn how to do that?" She then proceeded to introduce me to the concept of shielding.

Was I being too credulous in accepting that something unusual had happened, that day in the schoolyard? I can't say. In fourth grade,

I felt like a being caught between two worlds. There was this magickal existence where psychic phenomena were very real, a world of possibilities that was frightening in its enormity. I had caught glimpses of this world in books and on TV, as well as through my own experiences. I wanted desperately to believe in this magickal world, and yet I was afraid of that belief.

Did belief mean insanity? My great-aunt would say yes, and she would back up this assertion with her precious psychology, citing Freud and Skinner and countless other mysterious names. Even at that early age, I had a deep appreciation for my aunt's psychology as well as for hard science in its many guises. The world that stood in contrast to Pearl's magickal existence was the world of the five senses. This was the world of apparently adult thinking, where the only things that could exist were those that could be measured, reproduced, and boiled down in a beaker. Yet I was finding it increasingly difficult to reconcile my personal observations with the world that science and my teachers told me was out there. What should I believe?

In the midst of all these questions and confusions stood Pearl, humming tunelessly in a schoolyard in northeast Ohio, balls whizzing around her head and each one of them impossibly missing its target.

I decided to at least listen to what she had to say. I would walk into the world of magick with science still firmly set in my thinking. I would try her techniques, allowing myself to believe in their effectiveness for the duration of each experiment. If nothing happened, then I would revise my thinking. This was an approach that would serve me well in the coming years.

FIELD TRIPS

The only thing that allowed me to continue to take the whole dodgeball incident with a grain of salt was the humming. Pearl was quite convinced that she needed to hum that irksome, discordant note in order for the invisible shield to work. I could never bring myself to hum like that, dodgeballs or no dodgeballs. It always made me think that the next step might be putting aluminum foil on my head to block out the alien transmissions. But after that eventful afternoon, I did believe a little more in Pearl's abilities, which led ultimately to the lesson on dreamwalking.

We were on a field trip to some historic site in Ohio. I have no recollection of the site we visited, but the bus ride there and back is forever etched in memory.

In addition to myself, Pearl had one other "student" who was in our same grade. This girl, whom I'll call Jenny, was sick the day of the field trip and had to stay home. Pearl was worried about Jenny, fretting about her for most of the ride out to wherever we were going. This was in the days before cell phones, so of course Pearl had no way to check up on her friend from a distance. Finally, she started squirming around in the big green bus seat that we shared, apparently trying to lay down. This started to annoy me because she kept bumping me as I looked out the window at the passing trees. I'd almost banged my nose on the glass twice and I was not happy about it.

"What are you doing?" I finally demanded.

"Going to visit Celrim," came the response.

Celrim was Pearl's name for Jenny. In Pearl's world, everyone had at least two names. There was your birthname, which your parents gave to you. This name was useful in ordinary dealings, but it really didn't *name* a person. A person's real name was something Pearl called a "heartname." The heartname was a special name that only a few people were allowed to know. It still wasn't a person's true name, but it named them more truly than did their birthname. A person's teacher usually picked out the heartname. These days, we'd probably just call it their magickal name.

Celrim was Jenny's heartname. Pearl had given her this name earlier in the school year. Pearl's heartname was Jorna. Allegedly, Pearl's father, who was frequently absent from her life, had given her this name. Even though I was her student, Pearl refused to give me a heartname. Pearl insisted that I already had one, and that part of my learning would be remembering this name for myself. At the time, I thought this was a cop-out, and I was slightly jealous of Jenny's heartname. Why could Pearl name her other friend but not me? Years later, when the memory of the name finally did come, I understood a little more, and ended up reassessing a lot of things.

Heartname or no heartname, I couldn't see how Pearl was going to visit her ailing friend while riding a school bus through Central Ohio. I told her as much.

"I'm dreamwalking, silly," she replied.

As if that explained everything. Now, I had poured over that lone book on the paranormal that stood in the reference section of the school library, so I knew the basics of astral projection. People were supposed to have not one but two bodies, and one of these was made up of thought or energy. The astral body could be detached from the physical body, but it would always remain connected with a silver cord. As the book noted with an ominous turn, if the silver cord was ever cut, the person would die.

I had tried my hand at astral projection, ever mindful of that precious silver cord. Of course, I never had to worry about getting my silver cord cut or tangled, as I had no luck whatsoever detaching myself from my body. After several futile attempts, I concluded that astral projection was just a myth. According to the way I reasoned in those days, if I couldn't experience something for myself, then it wasn't real.

"So you're going to astral project or something?" I asked with a certain amount of derision.

Pearl—or Jorna, as I thought of her when she was engaged in anything particularly weird—frowned at me from behind her thick glasses.

"This is different," she said. "Why don't we try it together?"

I told her about my experiences, or lack thereof, with astral projection. She shook her head, as if dealing with a particularly thick-headed child, then proceeded to educate me on the differences between dreamwalking and astral projection. Like my heartname, she insisted that I already knew this and had just forgotten it. I wasn't sure I agreed with that assertion, but I kept my mouth shut. Pearl always seemed to think that I had forgotten more than I'd ever actually learned. In later years such statements would make a great deal more sense. However, back in the fourth grade, I was very certain of what I did and did not know. Dreamwalking was clearly in the "did not know" list. So I had Pearl explain it to me. In the course of that same bus ride, I also got a crash course in the concept of lucid dreaming.

Pearl first asked me if I remembered my dreams. I have always had a fairly rich dream-life, so I told her yes. Then she asked if I ever went flying in my dreams. These were in fact some of my favorite dreams, so again, the answer was yes.

"Do you visit people when you go flying in your dreams?" she asked.

"Well," I said. "I *dream* about them."

Again, that shake of the head, Pearl's universal gesture of impatience. After wrinkling her nose somewhat comically in thought for a few moments, Pearl finally asked if I'd ever become aware that I was dreaming during any of my dreams.

"Sometimes," I admitted. "Why?"

Pearl raised her eyes heavenward and asked no one in particular, "Why do I have to explain *everything*?"

Once she got over her annoyance at my thick-headedness, she continued the lesson. Lucid dreaming was important to the exercise we were about to undertake. It was the ability to become conscious of your dreams while you were still dreaming. Once you recognized that you were in fact dreaming, you could take control of events, chasing away the monsters in nightmares and even building the landscape of your own dreams. In dreamwalking, lucid dreaming was important because it not only allowed you to realize that you were dreaming but also enabled you to recognize the dreamspace as a real location, separated from physical reality, that you could then use as a gateway to other peoples' dreams.

This all seemed fairly complicated, and I wasn't really certain that I'd be able to master lucid dreaming *and* dreamwalking in one bus ride, no matter how ridiculously long it seemed. Pearl wrinkled her nose again at my objections and plunged blithely forward with our lesson for the day.

Once you recognized that dreams could be used as a gateway to travel from one dreamspace to another, all you had to do was reach out to someone you shared a connection with and "walk" into their dreams, she explained. The mechanism for this "walking" remained a little mysterious to me. Pearl insisted that you just thought about it and you were there. It seemed like wishful thinking to me.

"So how do I know I'm not just making up a dream where I dream that I'm walking into someone else's dream?" I asked in confusion.

Pearl once more wrinkled her nose and looked at me like I was being half-witted. Maybe I was.

"They'll remember the dream. That's why it's best to dreamwalk to people that you know," she explained. "They can tell you about the dream."

WOLf-DREAMS

For the next ten or fifteen minutes, we tried to relax enough to get into a lucid dream. I never fell asleep exactly, but later I learned that a dreamwalker does not have to be fully asleep. You can enter that borderline state between waking and sleeping and still successfully walk into other people's dreams.

Eventually, without losing my awareness of the bus around me, I saw in my mind's eye a pale figure wrapped in a blanket, lying on a couch. There was a coffee table nearby, scattered with a few books, magazines, and a half-empty glass of juice. The girl I was observing was Jenny—or Celrim, depending on which name one preferred to use.

"I see her!" I whispered excitedly. I did not open my eyes.

"You're just hovering around her," Pearl complained.

This time I did open my eyes.

"How did you know that?" I asked.

"I can see you, silly. Don't just look at where she's sleeping. Go and get into her dream."

It took a few moments to recapture the experience, but soon I felt like I was in two places at once again. I was conscious of my body on the school bus, head back, knees pressed up against the seat in front of me, jostling slightly as we traveled over a bumpy patch of road. Yet some part of me was also in Celrim's living room, looking down at her as she lay dozing on the couch. This part of me had no substance and seemed to stubbornly hang in midair, somewhere close to the ceiling.

"Don't do it that way. Get in the dream," said Pearl, and to this day I have no idea if I heard that command with my ears or with some other faculty.

"How?" I asked.

"You won't do anything just sticking around the ceiling like some ghost. *Dream.*"

Mentally, I shrugged and thought, *Here goes nothing.*

I willed it, as it had been explained to me, and then there was darkness. The darkness coalesced into a night sky filled with moon. There were stars and a field of glimmering snow, a distant forest denuded of leaves. Moving against the snow like a rolling tide of shadows was a pack of wolves. One of the wolves was bigger than the rest. Somehow, it seemed more real. It left the pack and walked toward us. It had a coat the color of moonlight, and big, luminous green eyes.

I thought I saw a shadowy figure bent near it, stroking its head. Things moved into dream-sense at this point. I knew, without knowing how, that the big silver wolf was Celrim. This was how she appeared in this place. The figure beside her, lavishing her with attention, was Jorna/Pearl. Pearl looked different in the dreamspace as well: prettier, a little older, her blonde hair longer than it was in waking life. She had no glasses. In this place, her eyes were as clear and luminous as the she-wolf's. Although she walked upright and still looked more or less human, there was something feline about her. Maybe it was the green eyes.

I didn't have a very strong sense of my own appearance in this dreamspace. If I looked at my hands, they appeared to be shadows. I felt vaguely unreal, and Jorna's ghost comment seemed entirely appropriate to me. It seemed like I was made of some weightless substance, dark yet transparent, and I felt just as I thought a ghost might feel standing in a room with embodied people. The wind in this place didn't blow past me so much as it seemed to blow through me, with a sensation like scattering leaves.

Uncertain what I should be doing, I just stood and watched Jorna whisper to her wolf friend. The whole "dream" lasted only a few heartbeats, I think. Even though it became very distant, I never lost awareness of my own body, and it was easy to shift my focus from the dream to where I still sat, scrunched down between the seats. I blinked and rubbed my eyes a few times.

"What did you see?" Pearl asked.

As was often the case with Pearl, she spoke without looking directly at me. Instead she was rummaging through her always full and always chaotic book bag for something. After a moment, she found what she was looking for and handed me a crumpled piece of notebook paper.

On it, she had drawn the face of a wolf. The picture was hardly the work of a master artist, yet I could see a slight resemblance between this rough sketch and the wolf I had seen in my "dream." Underneath the image of the wolf, Pearl had written something in her unmistakably scribbly handwriting: "Celrim."

Although I would experiment with this new skill for many, many years to come, in that moment, the part of me that Pearl was always trying to communicate with believed wholeheartedly in the reality of dreamwalking.

CHAPTER ONE

THE STUFF OF DREAMS

DREAMWALKING IS THE ART OF SENDING FORTH a part of the self in order to make contact with others through the medium of dreams. Anyone can learn how to dreamwalk, and, as we explore the concept throughout this book, you will find that most people probably already do. The trick, as with everything related to our internal, psychic worlds, is to bring this inborn talent into the realm of conscious control.

It's nearly impossible to find written material on dreamwalking. I maintain a library of several thousand books, and yet I do not own a single book on the subject. This is not for lack of trying; books on this topic simply do not exist. A survey of the Internet, moreover, is both flattering and frustrating: aside from references to Robert Jordan's *Wheel of Time* series, just about every entry on dreamwalking led me back to my own work in the *Codex*. And yet, dreamwalking is not a technique that I invented. It existed before this book, and it existed before I ever described it in *The Psychic Vampire Codex*.

The lack of available information on dreamwalking exists in part because there is no consistent nomenclature for the technique. There are accounts of dreamwalking mixed in with experiments in astral projection, dream telepathy, and lucid dreaming, but they are rarely identified as such. Other experiences, such as deathbed visitations and even some instances of psychic attack, could be classified as dreamwalking. Once again, however, these are rarely placed in a category that is separate and distinct. Many occultists from the nineteenth century onward have written volumes on astral projection and out-of-body experience, but if they address the intersection of these techniques with dreamwalking at all, it is only in passing. Of everything that has come down to us from the occult explosion of the nineteenth century, only one writer tackled the idea of dreamwalking head-on. His name was Hugh Calloway. He is better remembered by his pen name of Oliver Fox.

A WALK IN THE PARK

Hugh Calloway was a science and engineering student when he first began his studies of dreaming and the occult. Writing under the pen name Oliver Fox, he published a number of articles in the *Occult Review* and other esoteric journals around the beginning of the twentieth century. One afternoon, in the early 1900s, Calloway proposed a curious experiment to two of his friends. He suggested that they attempt to arrange a meeting later that night—in their dreams. For their meeting place, he chose Southampton Commons, a park that was well-known to all three of them. The other two young men, recorded as Slade and Elkington, agreed to make the attempt. So began one of the few recorded intentional adventures in the history of dreamwalking.

That night, Calloway dreamed of meeting with Elkington at the park. The two stayed around and chatted for some time, waiting for their third companion. Slade, however, never made an appearance. As they lingered in the dream-aspect of Southampton Commons, both Calloway and Elkington commented on Slade's absence. After a while, they grew tired of waiting, and left.

Calloway felt the experiment had been a success, and recorded his experiences for future readers. He contacted Elkington, and learned that his friend not only remembered dreaming of the Commons, he also recalled greeting Calloway remembered the distinct absence of Slade and how they both had commented on this in the dream.

Slade, for his part, felt the experiment had been a failure. When Calloway contacted him, he asserted that he had not dreamed at all that night. As far as Elkington and Calloway were concerned, this explained his absence at the park. As tantalizing as this little dream rendezvous was, Calloway writes that he was never able to reproduce it.

The young man remembered as Oliver Fox remains one of the few occultists to experiment with dreamwalking alongside his better-known work on astral projection. Most other occultists of his era preferred to explore the distant reaches of the astral plane, returning to tell vivid tales of their visits to the Akashic Records and the hallowed halls of the Ascended Masters. In many ways, it is easier to convince readers of extended forays into the astral realm than it is to convince them that one can travel to equally "real" places through dreams.

But this is the fundamental premise of dreamwalking: on some level, the dreamspace is real. It is not real in the sense that the physical world it real, but it is certainly as real as the astral planes described by writers like Madame Blavatsky and Dion Fortune. Like the astral planes, the dreamspace is a subjective reality. As much as it is a place we can go to, it is also a place that we shape with out hopes, desires, and fears. Not all dreams lead to this dreamspace, but the very act of dreaming opens up a gate that one can harness in order to enter this other realm of being. Because everyone dreams, even if they don't remember it, all of humanity can pass through the Gates of Dream and enter into the dreamspace. Skilled dreamwalkers do this intentionally, harnessing this twilight realm of shared imagery to communicate over long distances, reaching out to friends and family members in order to share an interaction that feels as real and immediate as anything carried out face-to-face in the waking world.

THE GOLDEN FLEECE

In the ancient world, it was believed that the realm of dreams connected the mortal world to the realm of the gods. Because of this, dreams were seen as the primary method by which the gods communicated with mortal men. In accordance with this belief, the kings of ancient Sumeria would ascend to the tops of their ziggurats and await a sacred dream that revealed the divine will. Some of the earliest known records of this kind of divine dreaming are clay cylinders that tell the story of King Gudea, ruler of Lagash, who sought the god Nin-Girsu in dreams. The Sumerian cylinders date to about 2200 B.C.E.

In Sumeria, contact with the gods through dreams was a privilege reserved for kings. By the time of the ancient Greeks, however, it was accepted that anyone could communicate with gods or daimons through the dreamspace. In a practice called "dream incubation," people would travel from all over to famous shrines and temples, seeking answers through dreams. These ancient dream-seekers would sleep in special dormitories, literally "sleeping houses," waiting for the gods to appear. In the most traditional method, the dreamer seeking counsel would lay out a sacred sheepskin, make the appropriate sacrifices, and then lay down on the sheepskin to go to sleep. A god, or a messenger of the gods, was then believed to appear to the dreamer in sleep. If the person was sick, the god would describe a cure for the illness. Others went to dream temples seeking advice on everything from career paths to marriage arrangements. As an interesting side note, the tale of Jason and the Golden Fleece is directly related to this practice. The fleece that Jason was charged to recover was a sacred sheepskin believed to be especially potent for this type of divination.

Dream incubation was not limited only to temples or shrines. A number of tombs in the ancient world were also considered ideal places to incubate. These included the tombs of the heroes Podalirius and Calchas in Apulia and the tomb of Trojan War veteran Achilles in Asia Minor. In these places, it was the spirit of the dead hero that appeared in order to communicate with the sleeper.

Just as the realm of dreams was believed to be accessible from the realm of the gods, the ancient Greeks also believed that the spirits of the dead inhabited a realm that intersected with the dreamspace. This belief that the dead can travel through the realm of dreams is not limited purely to the ancient world. Tibetan Buddhists developed a system called Dream Yoga that utilizes the similarities between the dreamspace and the Bardo, or spirit realm, to help a practitioner learn how to navigate the afterlife. Here in the West, one of the most common psychic experiences recorded among modern men and women is the deathbed visitation—a dream in which a loved one who has just passed away shows up to say goodbye. All of these traditions suggest that the Gates of Death and the Gates of Dream can both lead to the same place.

DEAD BUT DREAMING

Deathbed visitations are normally lumped in with ghostly phenomenon or with cases of proof of survival after death. However, they abide by all the rules of dreamwalking, with the possible exception that the person initiating the contact is dead. There is a long-standing belief that, once we die, all the mysteries of the Universe are imparted to us. This belief is the foundation of medieval necromancy, where magicians would conjure the spirits of the dead to lead them to buried treasure or to teach them secret wisdom that such individuals could never have known in life. Anyone who has dealt with spirits knows that the human dead do not, as a general rule, immediately ascend upon disincarnation. Quite the contrary, most human spirits are, in death, exactly the way they were in life, with the singular exception that they are no longer tied to a body.

That one small detail—the release from the physical body—has inspired the belief that death reveals some secret store of amazing wisdom to people. Death certainly *seems* to open up a whole host of abilities and perceptions. Ghosts communicate through empathy and telepathy. When they travel, they do so purely by an act of will, going from one place to another with little more than a thought. They have an innate sense of energy and a potent ability to interact with it. With sufficient effort, they can sometimes move physical objects. Their mere presence can change the temperature in a room, and they can often achieve a variety of electromagnetic effects, causing lights to flicker, turning appliances on and off, and even influencing recording devices. And, of interest to ancient Greeks and everyone reading this book, ghosts can also use the dreamspace to appear and communicate with the living.

Ghosts can do all of these things because they are beings of spirit, and spirit is energy. The punch line to the joke is that we're *all* beings of energy. The apparent difference in powers is not because ghosts have something we don't. Rather, the difference arises because they're lacking something that we have—a physical body to distract them from their subtler, spiritual side.

The Greeks were close in seeing the dreamspace as a point of intersection between the living and the dead, but their perception was a little skewed. The dreamspace *is* a crossroads, but not because it is the only place where the dead can cross over into the world of the living. In that space, spirits are still just beings of energy, no more or less "real" to us than they are in any other space. However, it is one of the few spaces where the living are also on equal footing with the spirits, obliged to interact beyond the context of the physical world.

Every night, our physical bodies shut down, and we are free to roam the pathways of mind and spirit. Most dreamers never reach out beyond their own internal realms, content to watch the play of images that results as their minds process information and experiences from the previous day. But we are all connected, even on the level of dreams. Psychologist Carl Jung observed this and called it the "collective unconscious." His contemporary, Sigmund Freud, observed that the mind is more receptive to psychic phenomenon in dreams. This is not to say that each and every dream leads us outside of ourselves to the dreamspace, but the gate is there, should we choose to walk through it.

SONGS BEYOND THE GRAVE

My maternal grandfather was an arresting figure of six foot eight, with a huge barrel chest and long rangy limbs. He was a man of many talents: a boxing champion in World War II, he was also a gifted dancer and a musician. Although I did not meet him until I was in my twenties, when we met, music was one of the things we bonded over. He was delighted to learn that, like him, I sang and played piano. When he passed away in the summer of 2004, his keyboard was the most important thing that he left to me. I had sworn to him that I'd play it, but of course, life can get overwhelming at times. I do a lot of things, and although I love music, I don't always find the time that I should to play. So, eight months after grandfather's death, his keyboard was still languishing in a corner.

Music was a talent that grandfather and I shared. Magick was another. Although he didn't always know what to call it, he worked magick every day of his life. As in music, he had no formal training in magick. He was gifted with something like the magickal equivalent of perfect pitch. Once he decided he wanted to do something, that's all it took. There was no theory, no spells, and no fancy terms. He would simply work his "mind over matter" with the same ease and proficiency that he would reproduce a song on the piano after hearing it once. Knowing this, I should not have been surprised when he showed up in my dreams to have a talk about the neglected keyboard.

The dream started out as exactly that—just a dream. I remember that it was night, and I was walking through a park in the city. I had come from a meeting of some sort and I was going to meet with some other people as a kind of follow-up. Both my point of origin and my point of destination were hazy, although they held great significance within the context of the dream. I think it all had something to do with books at a university library, forbidden knowledge, and some shadowy group of people seeking to uncover "the truth." That part of the dream seems trite, and might have had a lot to do with having read Dan Brown's *Angels and Demons* not long before. These details are really irrelevant to the overall experience, beyond the fact that they show that it started out as an ordinary dream—symbolic, but hazy, a little disjointed, and filled with a profound sense of meaning that becomes trite or elusive once it's translated into the waking world.

The thing that I recall most clearly is walking along the concrete path in the park. The night sky overhead was covered with clouds, and there were no stars. It would have been very dark, but old-fashioned street lamps with frosted orbs lit the way. It had to have been late fall in the dream because I could see trees just beyond the reach of the light, their branches naked and black against the sky. Writing it out now, it sounds terribly ominous, but there was no sense of menace in the dream. I often walk alone at night, and I find such a scene relaxing.

Time seemed to jump, as it so often does in dreams, and I found myself still walking along the same path, only now there was a building off to one side in the trees. The building was huge, styled like an old cathedral, complete with stained glass windows. There was light pouring through the windows, and people were going in and out of two big double doors on the side of the building. I knew, with that strange logic we encounter in dreams, that this was where I was supposed to meet up with the people I was going to see. I pulled my long camel-colored coat around me (a coat that I last owned in second or third grade), and headed into the cathedral-like building.

The inside of the building was bustling with people. Most of the main floor seemed to be a restaurant. There were tables everywhere, with richly-dressed patrons dining and sipping wine. I believe there was a fireplace against one wall, and everything was lit with candles or gaslight. The interior of the place had that warm glow that only living flame can convey. From this perspective, I could see the huge rose window that dominated the front of the building. It was done in rich blues and deep purples which, since it was dark out, looked almost black against the night. As the plot of the dream went, there was someone here I was supposed to meet, apparently so we could discuss whatever mystery had been uncovered at the university over dinner. I had just located his table and he was introducing me to two of his associates when something else captured my attention. This was a detail I had not noticed before, but when I did, it was like every other aspect of the dream became two-dimensional and indistinct.

Removed from the crowd of people socializing at their tables was a piano. It sat in an alcove away from and above the main floor. As soon as I noticed it, I was suddenly standing next to it. There was no movement. I was just there. And after that first moment of transition, the world of lamp-lit walkways, cathedral-like restaurants, and bookish mysteries just disappeared. I was in a wholly new space with plain cream-colored walls instead of stained-glass-covered walls of stone. The room was small, well-lit, and completely empty—except for the upright piano sitting before me. A man sat at the piano, playing. He wore a sleek black suit. His back was to me, so I couldn't see his face at first, but I could tell that he was an older gentleman. His neatly coiffed hair was gunmetal gray. Something about this person was so real and vivid that everything else leading up to this point of the dream seemed like—well, a dream. It was at this point that my dream became lucid—I was still dreaming, but I was aware of being in a dream.

Because I was now lucid dreaming, I tested my surroundings. I got the distinct impression that this person playing the piano was real, and that he had somehow invited me here—here being his little corner of the dreamspace. To check this, I tried changing various aspects of the dream. As lucid as I was, I could do nothing to either him or the piano. Since we were now the only two beings in this part of the dreamspace, I waited for him to finish what he was doing. Finally, as the last notes of the song faded away, he turned around to face me.

"Long time no see, granddaughter," he said with a grin.

He was younger than I remembered, but only slightly. Even at eighty-one, he had neither looked nor acted his age. We didn't hug. We didn't jump up and down, amazed to see one another again. There was no sense of urgency, although I was lucid enough to know that he was dead. When I mentioned this politely, he acknowledged the fact with a shrug. His death was a minor detail, hardly worthy of comment. My failure to play the keyboard he left me, however, was another matter entirely. He didn't exactly yell, but he scolded me gently, pointing out that if I waited to play the keyboard until I had some free time, I'd be playing it from his side of things.

At some point in our conversation, I made the excuse that I never know what to play. Grandfather, however, was prepared for this.

"I'll tell you what, granddaughter," he said. "There's just one song I really want to hear. So play *Give Me Back My Heart Again* and I'll stop pestering you about it."

"Is that even a song?" I asked. I'd never heard of it.

"Sure it's a song. Just look it up. My mother used to play it for me. We'd sit down at the piano and sing it together. *Give Me Back My Heart Again*," he repeated.

He mentioned the name of the song two or three more times, being insistent in his boyish "pretty please" kind of way. I woke up not long after that, the details of our meeting vivid in my memory.

HALLMARKS OF CONTACT

Whenever I have an unusual experience, I try to remain skeptical. Sometimes it's just too easy to see magick everywhere simply because you *want* to believe. My grandfather was one of the few members of my biological family who I was close to, so perhaps, psychologically, I was just conjuring him up in my memory because I missed him. I'd been too busy to think about either grandfather or his keyboard for a while, but unconsciously, I could have been feeling guilty about that. However, thanks to Pearl, I had been dreamwalking before my age reached double digits. I knew what a dreamwalk felt like, and this one had all the hallmarks I'd learned to look for. While it's good to question an experience from all possible angles, you should always trust your instincts. My instincts told me that this was more than just a dream, and the fact that it conformed almost exactly to an established type of experience backed that instinct up.

Grandfather's appearance had all the qualities of a classic dreamwalk. First of all, there was a pre-established connection between me and my grandfather. This was a bond of emotion as well as a familial tie. In almost every case of dreamwalking, whether it is intentional or unconscious, there is a link between the two people involved. We build ties like this between ourselves and the people who are important in our lives. Each time we talk with them and interact with them, the bond grows a little deeper. Such a link is evidenced by a growing rapport with the other person. How many people have had a best friend so close that they could finish that person's sentences for them? Some people think that links like this can last over lifetimes, creating soul-mates and soul-groups. If you've ever felt an immediate rapport with someone you just met, so powerful that you could finish their sentences just as if you'd grown up with them, it's possible that this is someone you knew in a past life. In meeting them for the first time now, you're really just picking up where you left off.

These links we forge with other people can be seen as tiny filaments of soul-stuff that connect us regardless of distance. In dreamwalking, these ties can help us find one another in the dreamspace, tracing the line back to its source.

The second detail that makes this a classic dreamwalk is the fact that I was both already asleep and already involved in my own dream before grandfather made contact. The person on the receiving end of a dreamwalk is almost always asleep. Typically, dreamwalkers interpose themselves into a pre-existing dream, although it is possible to shape elements of the dreamspace to create a specific setting that then serves as a backdrop for the interaction between both people in the dream. With grandfather, we saw how this worked. I had my own little Gothic mystery dream going and then there was the piano. The room that grandfather appeared in was separate and distinct from the previous dream, not only in terms of space but also in appearance and feel.

This leads right into a third detail that is very typical of dreamwalking experiences. The person being dreamwalked to often has a vivid recollection of the experience. Not only is the dream itself vivid, but it sticks with the person upon waking, and it seems to have both a greater clarity and a greater "reality" than an ordinary dream. It is also not unusual for the dreamwalking experience to be so vivid that it inspires some level of lucidity in the person being contacted. The irony with this is that often the person being dreamwalked to has an even clearer recollection of the experience than the person who initiated the dreamwalk in the first place.

Each of us has our own internal dreamworld, peopled with familiar objects, images, and themes. Although there is almost infinite variation, our dreamspace has its own cast of characters, and its own particular "feel." While we may not be able to put this "feel" into precise words, when something different interjects itself into our dreamspace, it creates a noticeable change. The person who initiates a dreamwalk has partial if not complete control over the setting and imagery of the dreamspace. Conscious dreamwalkers can put some effort into crafting a dream landscape, and over time, a kind of "inner temple of dreams" can be constructed that serves as the default for all interactions in the dreamspace. Otherwise, a neutral background that is very familiar to the dreamwalker will manifest itself. This is often one's childhood home, a space that is both comfortable and infinitely familiar. Other people have a comfortable outdoor location that they default to, like a lake or forest, which serves as the archetypal landscape of their dreams. Some people have a stock of several locales.

While this archetypal landscape is certainly familiar to the person initiating the dreamwalk, for the person on the receiving end, it will be strange. Even the most neutral backdrop will be memorable to the receiver simply because it is foreign to his or her dreams. In their 1970s research in dream telepathy at the Maimonides Medical Center, doctors Montague Ullman and Stanley Krippner concluded that dreams influenced by ESP could be identified by several factors. They were typically vivid, in full color, "somewhat puzzling to the dreamer," and they did not reflect any recent daytime activity. Just like with dreamwalking, the most significant identifier that the dream was something more than just a dream was the fact that it did not fit into the receiver's regular dream pattern. When images and actions are interposed into someone else's dreams, the very novelty of the material causes it to be remembered and remarked upon.

In the case of my dream about grandfather, the little room with the cream-colored walls and the upright piano was vivid and strange. It stood out in stark contrast with the rest of my dream landscape, which had an admittedly Gothic flair to it. Grandfather himself stood out from all the other characters of the dream. Not only was his presence foreign to the actual plot of the dream, but he also did not behave in accordance with the rules of my dreamspace. His very presence helped me achieve lucidity, and when I challenged him as nothing more than a dream, he asserted his own will in my dreamspace, making it abundantly clear that he could not be dispelled like some dream-phantom.

This points to a fourth characteristic typical of dreamwalking experiences. Not only is the experience vivid and memorable, but the interaction that occurred within the context of the dream feels *real*. Although I was aware that I had been asleep and dreaming, my little chat with grandfather at the piano felt exactly like any number of conversations we had had while he was still alive.

Not only did the communication *feel*, real, but what was communicated was accurate. Although it took a little digging, I finally found sheet music for *Give Me Back My Heart Again*. I'll admit, I got chills when I found it. A part of me still suspected that the experience might have just been a dream. However, the song grandfather was so insistent that I learn to play is a piece for voice and piano written in 1881. It's a romantic ballad composed by William Skuse with words by Linsey Lennox, and it's exactly the sort of thing I could see him sitting at the piano and singing with his mother, Victoria.

ROUNDED WITH A SLEEP

Our ancient ancestors attributed a great deal of meaning to dreams. Dreams were not just flickering images conjured by the mind. They were messages sent by the gods. They were a meeting ground for spirits, both human and otherwise. They could contain insights into the nature of reality, and they could contain insights into the nature of the self.

Thousands of years later, Sigmund Freud would reacquaint society with this meaningful approach to dreams. With the publication of his book, *The Interpretation of Dreams*, Freud founded the psychoanalytical movement, a branch of psychiatry that studies patients' dreams to learn the source of their troubles. Both Freud and his student Carl Jung brought dreams back from the wilderness of meaningless fantasy into the domain of profound insight.

Where Freud felt that our dreams were manifestations of our secret desires, Jung believed that dreams were manifestations of shared myths. Jung's concept of the collective unconscious, a layer of myth and symbol deep within each of our minds that connects all of us in mysterious ways, hearkens back to the ancient notions that the dreamspace is a realm unto itself, a hazy place of twilight where men can sometimes meet with gods.

My own experiences with dreams and dreamwalking have convinced me that dreams can serve an even greater purpose than revealing our unconscious urges and secret desires. While many dreams are certainly just dramas played out by the subconscious mind to integrate, enlighten, and instruct, some dreams have greater meaning still. Countless pages of psychical research from the nineteenth century and before are filled with experiences of prophetic dreams, dreams in which distant family members convey important messages, and *rêves à deux*—dreams that two people share.

All of these records suggest that there is another aspect to dreams. This is something that arises, spontaneously and uncontrolled for the majority of the populace, that draws upon a part of our minds that reaches beyond the limits of what we accept as normal, physical reality. Dreams can and do contain information that the sleeper should otherwise have no way of knowing. And sometimes, dreams allow individuals to close the distance between their physical bodies, meeting in a twilight realm of symbol and imagery that nevertheless allows for real interaction: *dreamwalking*.

We are such stuff as dreams are made on, and nowhere in the human endeavor is this more true than in the pursuit we call magick. Whether you are a witch, a psychic vampire, a magician, an energy worker, or merely a curious soul, the journey that lies ahead of you in this book is one of great relevance. Together we shall explore the undiscovered country of our dreams, and perhaps, by the end of this brief visit, we will have sketched out a map to help navigate future tours.

CHAPTER TWO

EXPLORATIONS AT THE EDGE OF SELF

ALTHOUGH I WAS TAUGHT DREAMWALKING at the tender age of nine, it was many years before I fully accepted it as a valid and real technique. That's not to say that I did not experiment with it in the interim. I had many experiences, intentional and otherwise, that strayed into the realm of dreams.

I grew up with a psychic grandmother who worked as a full-time "mom," her youngest brother, a salt-of-the-earth retired steel worker, and her oldest sister, a social worker who always yearned to be a full-fledged psychiatrist. The social worker, my great-aunt Rita, had a strong influence on me in those formative years. A devout Catholic, she was devoted to psychology with an equally religious fervor. Through her, I was exposed very early on to the works of people like Freud and Jung. The rules about reality that I learned from Aunt Rita often stood in stark contrast to my grandmother's frank discussions on psychic phenomena, not to mention my own experiences. Balancing between the two, I came away with a belief that extraordinary things were possible, but that the mind was also capable of tricking itself in extraordinary ways.

Rita worked at a state-funded psychiatric institute, and she was always telling colorful stories about her patients. My favorite story involved a patient known as "Superman." Superman, as the name suggests, believed that he was, in fact, the Man of Steel from the comic books. He was housed in the psychiatric institute because of this delusion, largely because he was considered dangerous to himself and others. The main danger he posed was the fact that he believed he could fly—a belief that eventually caused the institute to resort to physically restraining him.

The institution was an old building and most rooms had very high ceilings. Superman, as my aunt would tell it, would stand in the middle of the common area, announce that he was Superman to anyone who could hear, and then jump like a rocket to touch the ceiling tiles, which Rita estimated were about ten feet above the floor. This was no running jump, but a jump made from a standing position, straight up in the air. He didn't always succeed in touching the tiles, but sometimes he did. Sometimes he overshot and banged his head on them. "Superman" would also bend anything metal he could get his hands on and break other improbable objects in his efforts to prove that he was truly the Man of Steel.

My response, of course, was that maybe he decided he was Superman because he realized that he could do these extraordinary things. Rita admitted that this patient did exhibit extraordinary strength. It was hardly flight, but how many other people could go from a standing position and simply jump straight up to touch the tiles of a ten foot ceiling? In my aunt's opinion, however, the very fact that "Superman" was able to push his body past its ordinary physical limits was proof of his insanity. Because of his delusion, he didn't accept the normal rules that should govern his physical limitations; because of his delusion, he also could exceed those limits. To Aunt Rita, this was all simple psychology. To me, it verges on what many people describe as "magick."

Magick is the practice of imposing one's will upon reality in order to create change. The changes created by magick can take place in the outside world, but the most potent changes occur inside the self—changing attitudes, expanding abilities, pushing accepted limits—all through the exercise of willpower. Most traditional students of psychology, my aunt included, would deride magick as nothing more than delusion or wish fulfillment. And yet in that same breath, they will explain through the precepts of psychology how people can create amazing effects with sufficient belief. The real problem with magick is not that it's impossible to influence both internal and external worlds with mere thought—it's how subjective those thoughts can be in the first place.

SUBJECTIVITY, MIND, AND MAGICK

Magick is admittedly a subjective art. This is not to say that it is impossible to be objective about our experiences with magick. There are real, knowable laws that govern magickal techniques, or else they would not even take a similar form from practitioner to practitioner. The fact that we can go back through the writings of different individuals, different times, and different cultures and still see enough in common between reports to identify something even loosely under the term "astral projection," for example, says quite a bit. But magick, as we understand it, is a function of Will, and Will is something that is firmly rooted in the mind. This is one of the main reasons I will use the terms "magickal technique" and "psychic ability" almost interchangeably: magick, in many instances, is just an intentional application of psychic phenomenon.

When we are dealing with phenomenon in the physical world, such as chemical reactions, it is possible to measure and quantify what is going on. One can reliably take a small amount of baking soda, hand it over to someone else along with a vial of vinegar, and show very clearly how these two things interact. It is harder to take the experience of a telepathic dream, extract the details wholesale from the mind, and hand it over to another person so he or she can experience that dream in precisely the same detail.

We cannot put something like that into a vial to measure it. We have neither the tools nor the language to begin to quantify it. This does not just involve paranormal phenomenon: the same problems arise when we try to quantify thoughts or emotions. When a person experiences a particular thought, one might be able to measure some of the related chemicals or electrical impulses in the brain, but these things can only tell us that *something* is going on. An EEG can reliably tell us when someone is dreaming, but only the dreamer can tell us what that dream was about.

Magick or psychic experiences are hard to quantify because most of the work takes place in the mind, where few methods can measure or capture it. Furthermore, these experiences are subjective because each person perceives and interprets the world in a different way. When we dream, we each have our own unique set of symbols, developed and based upon experiences throughout our lives. Similar sets of symbols and associations are at work whenever we process a mental experience. As a simple example, my thoughts tend to manifest in words and images. Another person may think more in terms of feelings. A third may have mental processes more akin to numbers and code. If we work from nothing more than this one principle, all three people described above could think suddenly, "I'm hungry," yet experience that thought very differently in their internal worlds.

Radically different senses, symbols, and metaphors can be chosen by each person, but in the end, it's the same thought. Our point of perception influences the manner in which that perception is expressed—both internally and externally. This is a basic principle in psychology, and it is the principle at work in all the most confusing manifestations of reports about magickal and psychic techniques. However, this subjective quality to magickal experience does not prevent us from taking a rational and systematic approach to such experiences. In many ways, it means that we must be even more diligent in how we study, analyze, and record those experiences, so that greater understanding can be had by all. The key in magick, as in science, is repeated and consistent experimentation—and the willingness to revise and adapt our theories about the workings of the universe as new experiences present themselves.

THE STARING GAME

There is a hazy line separating "mind over matter" from "it's all in your head." Because of my upbringing, this line is of particular interest to me. As gifted as I have been with psychic abilities, I have nevertheless been driven repeatedly to verify them and understand them in the context of history, psychology, and science. Dreamwalking is no different. One of the reasons I think many occultists have stayed away from dreamwalking is because the realm of dreams is so very subjective. Aside from unusual instances where there is some key detail that can be used to validate the experience, we are often left wondering if the experience was real or truly just a dream. Coming from the background that I did, I could not take Pearl's instruction at face value. No matter how successfully the technique seemed to work, I needed to prove to myself that it wasn't just some mental trick.

The Universe has always had a sense of humor with me. As abruptly as events had conspired to put me in a class with Pearl, by the end of that school year, we were separated. My own school had started up a gifted program, and so there was no further need to ship me out on a thirty minute bus ride in order to attend Pearl's school. I learned a lot of very strange things in that year at Sharon Elementary, but by fifth grade, I was on my own again. Without Pearl's instruction, I was left to puzzle things out on my own. For the background on the techniques that Pearl had touched upon, I started devouring books on psychic phenomenon. In order to put the experiences into some kind of context that I could accept, however, I couldn't just rely upon books. I needed to experiment.

By sixth grade, my best friend in all the world was a girl we'll call Katie. Collectively nicknamed "the giggling girlies" by her father,

Katie and I were inseparable. We spent hours on the phone together, and when we could wheedle our parents into consenting, we would have sleepovers that stretched out across whole weekends. Katie and I were the kind of friends who could finish one another's sentences without even thinking about it. When one of us was having a bad day, the other knew, and on a few occasions, it seemed that we had dreamed the same thing in the same night.

One of the things that Katie and I did on a regular basis was have staring contests with one another. I can't explain why it amused us so much, but we would spend hours staring intently into one another's eyes until the other finally blinked. The rules were simple. You had to stare into the other person's eyes, and if you blinked, you lost. However, so long as you maintained an unbroken gaze, you could do whatever you wanted, short of blowing into the other person's face, in an attempt to get that person to laugh, blink, or look away. Usually, we would just make grotesque faces at one another, trying to get the other to laugh so hard that she had to look away.

Fairly early on in our little game, I discovered that if I stared long enough into Katie's eyes, her face would start to blur and change well beyond her own ability to distort it. I knew enough about biology to understand that some of this was just my eyes getting tired. If you stare fixedly at the same point for long enough, you fatigue the receptors and, among other things, your perception of color can shift. But sometimes, as I watched her features rearrange themselves on her face due to eye fatigue, I would get brief flashes of images. These were independent of her face and seemed almost to hang on the air between us—as if, by looking at her until my eyes couldn't see anymore, I ended up looking into an entirely different space.

I didn't talk about it at first because I had no idea what was going on. Usually, the images seemed like nonsense anyway—a bird, a doll, some unfamiliar outdoor scene. But then, days or weeks later, something would come up in conversation and Katie would mention something she had been thinking while we were having our staring contest. In many cases, it was related to the images I had seen.

What started out as a silly game eventually turned into a potent tool for building and utilizing the connections between people. By staring fixedly at the same point while simultaneously trying to put ourselves in a mindset where no outside distraction could break our gaze, we were putting ourselves very naturally into a trance state. Since we were focusing so intently on one another, this trance state was building on that focus, allowing the transmission of thoughts and images, albeit unconsciously. So, I thought to myself, what happens if one of us tries to send images intentionally?

THE WORLD IN YOUR EYES

Here is where I admit that, at least to begin with I did not tell Katie that I was experimenting on psychic phenomenon with her. This is not exactly ethical, but it seemed like the only way to make certain that something real was going on. If I told Katie before we sat down to our staring contests that I was going to try transmitting images to her, she would begin to look for them. Sometimes, just by holding the expectation that something should occur, we stop looking objectively at our experiences. It's like that old game where someone tells you, "Don't think about white elephants," and suddenly, all you can think about is white elephants. Only in this case, you're not just thinking about white elephants—you're looking at things that are not at all white or elephantlike and still trying to see how they *might* be white elephants. When we've been set up with a specific expectation, our minds become selective in how they interpret data, often skewing our interpretations unconsciously to meet or frustrate the expectation.

This was one of the main reasons I was skeptical about so many of my experiences with Pearl. For example, when she was trying to get me to receive telepathic messages, she would make it obvious that she was concentrating on something. When I wouldn't immediately comment, she would ask me something like, "Did you get my message? The one about the tree?"

With a question like that, it was impossible to remain objective about the experience. When she was staring at me like she was trying to send me a telepathic message, quite a number of things would pass through my mind. One of these things might have involved trees, but how could I be certain that I hadn't just simply been thinking about trees?

With Katie, I was determined to keep things as objective as possible. We had been having staring contests all along, and so nothing to her would change. However, on my end of things, I would focus on sending something while we were having the staring contest. I would give no indication what this was or even that I was attempting to send it. I would simply wait for Katie to remark upon it. If Katie accurately perceived what I was attempting to transmit without any prompting from me, then I could be satisfied that it wasn't just one or the other of us trying to interpret things in order to meet expectations.

The first few times I tried this, I focused on an object. I fixed the image in my mind, and as we stared eye to eye, I concentrated on sending an image of the object to Katie. There were a couple of times where Katie would shake her head and say something like, "That's funny. I'm thinking about my doll's house all of a sudden." I had been sending an image of one of her dolls, so the impression was close, but not perfect.

Even though we had a few reasonably close hits, I still wasn't satisfied with these experiences. How could I know that Katie didn't just happen to start thinking about her doll's house on her own? It was a fairly prominent item in her life. Most of the objects I chose to focus on were normal, everyday things, and there was always a possibility that Katie just happened to think about them around the same time I was trying to send the images to her. We were right back at the quandary about trees. Then there were the many instances where I sent something and Katie made no unusual comments to indicate that she had received anything. The frustrating thing about this was also related to the commonplace nature of the images. I had been "seeing" images during our staring contests for quite some time, but because they were images of fairly normal things, I never felt the need to talk about them. Katie could have been doing the same thing, mistaking the images for her own stray thoughts or simply ignoring them. If I wanted to continue the experiments without telling her about them, then I needed to come up with something simple enough to transmit clearly but remarkable enough that there would be no doubt if or when it was received.

When I stared eye to eye with Katie, it often felt as if our eyes were a gateway, and somehow we were traveling through them to a place beyond our physical bodies. That notion seemed silly the first time it occurred to me, but it stuck with me, and I decided to use it, no matter how strange or crazy it sounded at the time. After limited success with transmitting images of objects (I had tried moods and emotions at one point as well, but abandoned them quickly due to how very subjective they could be), I hit upon creating a landscape. It couldn't be a place that Katie or I knew in the real world. It had to be completely unique, and clear enough that its details would stand out to her, driving her to comment on them. I would imagine that my eyes were the gate to this landscape, and as Katie was staring at me, I would try to pull her through to my imagined landscape.

I imagined a landscape at night, with an old, dead tree off to one side and more leafless trees in the background. A huge full moon hung in the sky. Before I tried experimenting with this image with Katie, I imagined it over and over again in my mind. I tried to make it as real as possible, picturing it as if it were an actual place that I could go to. I even drew it, making a detailed picture of my eye and part of my face, with the landscape visible through the pupil. Once I could imagine the landscape clearly and consistently, then I felt I was ready to try sending the image to Katie.

I was sleeping over at her house that night. We had been sitting on her bed as we always did, talking about all kinds of things and giggling away. There was a tickle fight or two mixed in there, and this eventually led to the usual round of staring contests. I situated myself across from her on the bed, crossing my legs under me and getting comfortable. Before we started, I closed my eyes and mentally put myself in the landscape I had created. With the image of the tree and the moon and the night sky firmly in mind, I raised my head and met Katie's eyes.

Maybe it was the serious way I had started, but this contest felt different from many of the others right from the beginning. There was none of the usual giggling and horseplay. Instead, we sat opposite one another, perfectly silent, staring eye to eye. Neither of us moved. We barely breathed. The world narrowed down to the focus of our eyes and the space between. Almost immediately, I experienced that sense of being pulled into some other direction of reality, where our bodies remained sitting and staring at one another but our minds were elsewhere. This other place was even closer than our bodies, which sat on the bed, knee to knee.

Still focused on Katie's eyes, I concentrated on my landscape. I imagined that I could somehow reach into Katie's eyes with my own, pulling her through our pupils like they were a gate, to this other space that I had created. I wanted her to experience the landscape as clearly as I was experiencing it, as if it were a real place hanging in this non-space between our focused, staring eyes.

Katie broke the gaze. Her eyes went wide for a moment and she actually jumped back a little.

"Oh my God," she swore. "I saw, like, a moon in your eyes."

"You did?" I asked, moving as little as possible and continuing to focus on her eyes. I continued to focus on the landscape, having this strange sense of double vision as I simultaneously sat on the bed before her and remained standing by the tree in the moonlight.

Katie still seemed startled, and she had initially pulled away. However, now she leaned closer, peering into my eyes again.

"It's weird," she said, "but it's like I can still see it."

Excited, I decided to break the rules of the experiment just a little bit.

"What else do you see?" I asked softly, focusing even harder with my eyes.

Katie obliged by slipping right back into the staring-contest pose, gazing deep into my eyes and losing herself there.

"It's dark," she whispered. "And there's this huge, white moon."

I waited expectantly for her to go on. This was better than I had imagined it could be.

Finally, she said, "And I think you're standing by a tree. Isn't that weird? I feel like I'm in two places at once."

Our staring contests were forever changed. I let Katie in on what I had been doing, and subsequent sleepovers would find us sitting on her bed, staring intently at one another, describing in soft voices what we could see in the space created by our gaze.

INNER TEMPLE OF DREAMS

I didn't realize it at the time, but I had hit upon a technique that is essential to dreamwalking. In creating that simple moonlit landscape, I made a kind of "inner temple of dreams." This was my dream haven, a space removed from the physical world that I—and others—could access through visions and dreams. Although it started off as a mental construct, shaped with my imagination, it nevertheless had enough intent behind it to be, on some level, real. After stumbling upon this technique with Katie, I expanded on the concept in subsequent years, learning not only how to shape an internal landscape but also shaping my appearance in that mental place.

One of the first steps in learning how to dreamwalk does not take place in dreams at all—at least, not at first. Before you begin journeying in the realm of dreams, it's a good idea to have a starting point. Crafting your personal dream haven gives you a staging ground that can lead into the dreamspace. It is a place that is totally your own, designed and created by you, carried within so you can access it no matter where you may be in the waking world.

MAKING A DREAM HAVEN

Your dream haven is an internal space defined and shaped by your imagination. Your first trips to your dream haven will be done during meditation, while you are awake. The dream haven will remain a space that you can reach while awake and meditating, but it will also serve as your starting point each time you seek to enter the dreamspace. You can also use your dream haven as your default landscape when dreamwalking, reaching out to others and drawing them from their dreams into your personal imagined landscape. You don't have to use your dream haven in this capacity, however. You can keep this space completely private, if that's what you want, using it as a kind of staging ground that opens up onto other, more elaborate or more public dream landscapes.

The first step to building your dream haven is deciding exactly how it should appear. You dream haven can be anything or anywhere. It can be a real place that has significance to you, or it can be a completely imaginary space, perhaps inspired by a book or even a movie. Your dream haven can be in a house or in a temple, located high up on a mountain or nestled beside a smooth, calm lake. One friend of mine imagines a crystal palace suspended in the void of space. Because you are building this space with your imagination, your imagination is your only limit. If you're having trouble coming up with ideas, take some time to sort through old photos to see if there is a place there that feels right for your dream haven. Alternately, you can look through books with pictures of landscapes or buildings, or watch movies for sources of inspiration.

What you are seeking is a space that has meaning to you, a space where you feel comfortable, centered, and safe. It is a space that is removed from your everyday reality, so it should have some qualities that remind you of the dreamspace. It should also be a space that is relatively simple to imagine. It does not have to be stark, but you need to be able to picture the image clearly in your mind. Keep in mind that you will be using your imagination to build each item and detail of this space. If you want something elaborate, focus on something simple first, and then add to it once you have the basic image in mind.

Your dream haven should not be immense. Rather, focus on a space no more than twenty feet in diameter. This is about the size of a large room. This is a manageable size, small enough so you can control each detail, but not so small that you will feel cramped. If you have decided on an outdoor landscape, be sure to define the limits of this space. A sunny hillside does not have walls like a room, but there can be a wall of trees ringing it around, defining the space. Alternately, you can have the space simply fade away after a certain point, so that your dream haven is ringed with mist. This can help to give it an other-worldly feel, subconsciously reminding you that your private dream haven can connect to many different places.

Once you know what you want your dream haven to look like, you should have an image you can focus on. If you are artistic, then you can make a sketch of your dream haven. If you have built your dream haven upon images from books or old photographs, keep these handy to focus upon. If you have no good visual representation of your dream haven, write out a description, making the details as vivid as possible. Spend some time, either looking at the image of your proposed dream haven or reading the description of your dream haven out loud. Once you have done this to fix the details of this space in your mind, then you are ready to build it through visualization.

Set sometime aside in your day so you can be alone and undisturbed. Sit back in your chair or on your bed, close your eyes, and imagine your dream haven. You might want to put on some music to help you get into a meditative state of mind. If you have trouble concentrating on the image at first, take a few minutes to look back over the photo or reread the description you've written down. As you concentrate on the picture or the description, fix the image in your mind. Holding the image as clearly as you can, close your eyes once more and picture it as a real landscape in your mind.

You may want to focus on each single detail at a time. For example, in the dream haven I accidentally created with Katie, the first thing I really pictured was the old dead tree. After that had become fixed in my mind, then I focused on the moon in the sky. The rest of that dream haven followed logically from these two images. The more I worked with it, the more solid it became. Eventually, it seemed as if it was a real landscape that I could walk to whenever I closed my eyes.

It will take time to build your dream haven, so be patient with yourself. This is not something that you will be able to create in just one sitting. Also, don't make the mistake of assuming that the longer you focus, the more successful you will be. In my own practices, I have found that short periods of meditation repeated frequently are far more productive than one long marathon session. Spend five or ten minutes at a time imagining your dream haven as clearly as you can, and then take a break. Just be sure to keep at it, repeating the exercise several times throughout the week.

Don't try too hard and don't overdo it. The key is to simply keep at it. Whenever you have some spare time, call the image to mind with as much detail as possible. The first few times that you try to build your dream haven, you may find that you *must* have a quiet and controlled environment to meditate in. However, there is nothing stopping you from closing your eyes in class or taking a few moments out of your workday to picture this image in your mind. Calling the image of your dream haven to mind in class or at work serves a double purpose. First, if you can imagine the landscape clearly even in a mundane environment surrounded by distractions, then you will know that it is becoming very solid in your imagination. Secondly, since this is a safe and comfortable internal space, visiting it in class or at work can give you a break from the "real world," providing a quiet, private space where you can recharge no matter where you really are.

You have been successful in building your dream haven, if:
- You can call it to mind at will
- All of the details appear vividly without concentration
- It feels like a real space that you carry within your mind

BUILDING A GATE OF DREAMS

The Gates of Dream are an archetypal image that I return to again and again in this book. Archetypes and symbols have some objective reality within the realm of dreams, and the Gates of Dream represent the point of passage from your personal dreams to the wider territory of the dreamspace. You can harness this archetypal image in your dream haven, creating a crossing-over point that can later serve as a focus for when you seek to dreamwalk.

In the previous exercise, you spent some time crafting an internal landscape to use as your personal dream haven. This space, built through imagination, nevertheless verges on the territory of dreams. You have set boundaries defining this space, and now it is time to build a portal that can take you beyond the boundaries of your private landscape.

What do you think about when you read the words, "The Gates of Dream?" Is there an image that comes immediately to mind? Focus on this image until it becomes more distinct. If you haven't put an image to the concept of the Gates of Dream yet, take some time to craft it. What would a gate that opens up onto the realm of dreams look like? Is it an ancient doorway, inscribed with runes that glow when you invoke its powers? Is it a tear in space that hangs in the air, shifting and shimmering? Perhaps it is a well, and by gazing into its waters you can see other people and places. By diving in, you can travel to what you see. As with everything in your dream haven, you are limited only by your imagination. Your primary concern is that the image of your dream gate should appeal to you, really resonating with its purpose and function. Remember that this is a gate that not only leads into the subjective space of dreams—it is also a gate that verges on the realm of spirits and even the realm of mythic gods.

When you have a good idea of how the Gates of Dream appear to you, draw the image or write out a vivid description. Focus on this for a little while, reading over your description or studying the image. Finally, when you have the image of your personal take on this gate firmly fixed in your mind, go to your dream haven. Once you are in your dream haven, walk to an area that is removed from the rest of the haven. You may have to create this area as you do so. If your dream haven is in a building, walk a short distance away from the main area and then open a door that leads to a new room. This room can be completely empty. In some ways, it's more helpful if you perceive this new space as a blank slate, totally unworked until you walked in.

If your dream haven is located out of doors, find a path that leads you to a far edge of the central space. This path leads to a clearing, removed from the main area of your dream haven. This clearing should also be a new space, completely unworked and unembellished. When you arrive at this new portion of your dream haven, whatever form it takes, begin crafting your personal dream gate. You can craft it by simply calling it into existence, whole and complete, or you can craft it piece by piece with the stuff of dreams. Shape the gate according to the image you have compiled, using whatever means seem most productive to you within your dream haven. The dream gate should stand in the middle of the new, clear space and it should be the main thing in this space — if not the only thing.

When you are done crafting your dream gate, take some time to just study it, making it a real object within your dream haven. This is your portal into the dreamspace. When dreamwalking, you can pass through this portal to other people's dreams or you can draw them through the portal to you. Focus not just on the appearance of this dream gate but also focus on its identity as a crossing-over point. This is the threshold that leads you from one space to the next, and your desire is the key to where it leads.

My dream gate is a huge portal, edged in ivory and horn. Stretched between the pillars of ivory and horn is a surface of swirling mist. My dream gate stands alone in a remote clearing in my dream haven, raised up on a little hill of tightly packed earth. When I focus on someone, the mist clears and I can see them standing on the other side of the gate. Their image helps me focus on the connection between us, and when I feel that connection strongly enough, I reach out to that person, either walking through the dream gate to join them on the other side or tak-ing their hand and pulling them across into my space.

Just as you built the landscape of your dream haven piece by piece over successive meditations, use successive meditations to fix the form and function of your dream gate in your mind. Spend five or ten min-utes at a time imagining the gate in the new section of your dream haven, then take a break. Once the gate seems solid enough, take some time to focus on the gate as a connecting point, looking through to other places or calling up images of the people you are connected to. Don't walk through just yet. Simply acquaint yourself with the notion that this is a gate and that it leads from your dream haven to other points in the dreamspace.

You have successfully crafted your dream gate, if:

- It manifests clearly without any effort
- It is something you can physically pass through/into
- You can use it to connect to others
- You perceive it as a gate leading beyond your dream haven

CRAFTING YOUR EIDOLON

"Eidolon" is a Greek word meaning idol or image. Most often associ-ated with ghosts, a person's eidolon was the image or shade that man-ifested after death, but it could also sometimes fly forth in dreams. Within the context of the dreamspace, your eidolon is the image that you project. When dreamwalking, we naturally present an image of ourselves. This is typically an unconscious image of how we think we look. If we do not consciously craft an eidolon, we will default to this unconscious image of ourselves. However, it is possible to put some thought into how we appear in the dreamspace. Crafting your eidolon has a number of benefits. The primary benefit in crafting your eidolon is that you have a much more solid presence in the dreamspace.

Crafting your eidolon is a fairly simple process. The first thing you need to do is simply decide how you want to present yourself in the dreamspace. If you had to pick the most archetypal image of you, how would it look? What type of clothes do you typically wear? What does your hair look like? Would you be wearing glasses? Would you have anything with you, besides just yourself? Some of us have an item that is so important to us in our lives that it has almost become an extension of who we are. Appearing without this item feels almost like being naked. For me, there is a ring I wear with a stone of black onyx. I've had the ring for so long that it has actually changed the shape of my finger, and I could not imagine my hand without it. Many of us have items like this that have become such a part of our self-image that, without them, we're incomplete.

Take a few moments to think about the answers to these questions. If you're artistic, draw a picture of how you ideally look. If, like myself, you're no Michelangelo, then sort through all of your photos until you find one that seems to perfectly represent you. Spend some time studying this photo, really fixing the image in your head. Alternately, you can sit in front of a mirror for a little while, studying your face, your eyes, your hair, and so forth. Be certain to pay attention to more than just your face, otherwise only your face will be focused and clear in the dreamspace, while the rest of your body may appear indistinct.

Once you have an image that you are pleased with, spend some time meditating upon it. Put yourself in your dream haven, and concentrate on your appearance. Remember: this image is not meant to be a projection. Think of it instead as a kind of glamour you wear while in the dreamspace. The image is not separate from you but builds upon what is already there.

Standing in your dream haven, look down at yourself, keeping the desired image clearly in mind. Run your hands down your face imagining that, as you do, your features conform more perfectly with the ideal image you have in mind. Run your fingers through your hair, shaping it in accordance with the desired image as well. Feel your body around you, and everywhere your hands pass, watch as your appearance solidifies, coming more clearly into focus and shifting to match the ideal image in your mind.

Once you have imposed your ideal image on yourself in the dream space, take some time adjusting to this eidolon. Examine the clothes that you're wearing. If you're wearing glasses, reach up and feel them on your face. If you're having trouble seeing yourself in your dream haven, imagine that there is a mirror in the space you have crafted. Make this a full-length mirror, so you can see yourself from head to toe. Then, just as you spent time imagining your dream haven over and over again, put some time into seeing yourself in that space as you wish to be seen. Stand in front of the mirror, and study yourself from head to toe, until you have a solid and clear image of your eidolon. Focus on what it feels like to be in that space, wearing that appearance. Interact with the other objects in your dream haven, reaching out your hand to touch things and studying your fingers, the length of your arm. Your goal is to attach the eidolon firmly to your sense of "you" in the dream haven so when you move on to dreamwalking, this will be how you appear in the dreamspace.

You have successfully crafted your eidolon, if:
- You identify the image as you
- The image provides a point of first person perspective
- The important details manifest automatically
- It feels just like your physical body

These are just the basics of what you can do when consciously crafting your eidolon. For more advanced techniques, see chapter ten, "Sex in the Dreamspace."

EYES WIDE OPEN

If, like me, you have a particular passion for verifying your experiences, then once you have completed these three preliminary exercises, you can recreate my experiments with Katie. Find a partner who is willing to participate. Spend some time crafting both your eidolon and your dream haven. Write clear descriptions of these down and keep them some place safe. Do not share these descriptions with your partner.

Find a place that is quiet where you will not be disturbed. Sit across from your partner. Make sure that you're both comfortable, then begin by locking eyes. Sit and gaze at one another in silence, staring fixedly eye to eye. As you stare at your partner, let your mind travel to your dream haven. Be aware of your partner and maintain eye contact, but at the same time, vividly imagine your dream haven around you. If you can, envision yourself in both places as once: seated in front of your partner, gazing, and also standing or otherwise interacting with the landscape of your dream haven.

Think of your eyes as the physical representation of your dream gate. Call up a clear image of your dream gate in your mind and overlay your perception of this gate with your perception of your partner's eyes. Imagine that your pupils are the other side of the gate, the side your partner can perceive and walk through. This can be tricky, because it requires you to essentially see two things at once, interacting with these two layers of perception as if they were one thing.

Now, holding this delicate balance of perception in your mind, reach through the dream gate and connect with your partner. Feel the energy of your partner; connect on the level of pure essence. When you feel that you have established this connection, mentally invite your partner to join you in your dream haven.

In order to be strictly objective, have your partner write down anything that he or she perceives. Share your description of the dream haven only if your partner has succeeded in perceiving a significant number of the details related to that space. Otherwise, simply let your partner know if any of the details were right and try again. When assessing the accuracy of the perceptions, try not to give your partner leading comments.

Your partner should also craft an eidolon and a dream haven and record descriptions of these. After you have tried bringing your partner into your dream haven, switch roles and have your partner try letting you in. From this perspective, make an active effort to travel inward, interposing your partner's eyes with your dream gate. Record any images or impressions that you perceive.

It is very likely that you will encounter difficulty with this exercise at first. However, don't give up. It is also just as likely that there will come a particular moment when everything shifts and the images come clearly for both of you. If you manage to achieve such a level of connection, then by all means take advantage of it. Practice shaping dream landscapes by altering things within your dream haven and seeing what your partner can pick up on. As you work with the same partner over and over again, you will build a rapport that will prove very helpful when you move into full dreamwalking. It is possible to achieve a level of connection where you and your partner are essentially dreaming wide awake, so you both remain conscious of sitting across from one another, staring eye to eye, but at the same time, you can perceive the projected places and images around you, able to interact with them by intent alone.

Even if you never achieve that level of perception in this exercise, any feedback you can get on your dream haven or your eidolon will help build confidence in your ability to shape and project these things within the dreamspace.

CHAPTER THREE

THE SHIFTING BOUNDARIES
OF DREAM

IN MOST TYPICAL DREAMWALKING SESSIONS, two people are involved, although there is no defined limit to how many people can participate together in the dreamspace. In general, however, a standard dreamwalk involves just two. One of these people is the active participant while the other serves as the receiver.

The active participant is the one who initiates the dreamwalk, willfully reaching out to and connecting with the receiver. It is the active participant who initiates most of the action in the dreamspace. The active participant also helps define that dreamspace, consciously or unconsciously bringing elements into the imagery and landscape of the dream.

People on the receiving end of a dreamwalk do not have to be wholly passive. In the most ideal situation, both parties are aware of the dreamwalk and are actively working to connect in the dreamspace. However, there are cases of spontaneous dreamwalking where even the active participant may not be consciously aware of dreamwalking.

Dreamwalking, although it can be guided by the conscious mind, is an activity that is directed largely by the subconscious. The subconscious mind is like a stranger inside of you who's running the show. The subconscious mind stores memories that your conscious mind—

the "you" that you think of as "you"—has no access to. It knows more about what drives and motivates you than you'll ever know, and sometimes it even intentionally hides things from you. In extreme cases, it can create whole other personalities that sometimes come to the forefront to deal with difficult issues, while "you" remain ignorant of what they say and do.

Although the two minds are connected (they are, after all, parts of the same person), it's as if they speak very different languages. Trying to mediate communications between the conscious and subconscious minds is a challenge that has been the focus of much of modern psychology, particularly the discipline known as psychoanalysis. Establishing open communications is a very difficult undertaking, because, by definition, the subconscious mind is largely unknown and unseen to our waking selves.

As a result of this connection to the subconscious, volition and control can be very tricky issues in dreamwalking. The active participant in a dreamwalking session can choose a target who is neither aware of the activity nor consenting to it. This raises a number of ethical concerns that we will address later in this book, and it's why some forms of dreamwalking can be considered psychic attacks.

Most dreamwalking sessions occur when both parties involved are asleep, or at the very least have reached the threshold state between waking and sleep—otherwise known as the hypnagogic state. There have been cases where a dreamwalker has successfully made contact with an individual in the waking world, however. When the person on the other end of a dreamwalk is awake, the interaction that ensues typically takes the form of a daydream or vision, phenomena that seem to ultimately occupy the same psychic realm as ordinary dreams.

In most dreamwalking experiences, there is rarely a sense of travel between the dreamwalker and the person being dreamwalked to. Even when one dreamwalks from the hypnagogic state, the process seems distinct from etheric or astral projection. Rather than sending a part of the self out to explore this or other worlds, the dreamwalker focuses on a person and travels inward, through dreams. The lines between dreamwalking and astral projection can be hazy, however, especially if the target of a dreamwalk happens to be awake.

CALIFORNIA DREAMING

While running an event at a convention in 1995, I met an amazing friend. A first generation Chinese American, his family had imported a style of energy work to the West and ran a Qi Gong clinic in Modesto, California. He makes an appearance in my book, *Sacred Hunger*, because he was able to pick up on some unique qualities in my energy body just from sight. I called him "Casey" in that book, and for the sake of consistency, I'll stick with that pseudonym here.

Casey and I were each excited about our own particular methods of energy work, and whenever we had a chance to work together in person, we often experimented with a variety of things. His favorite game was to see how much energy he could channel, and how much I could take. Because we lived nearly 2500 miles apart, our chances to work together face-to-face were few and far between, limited mostly to those times when we both attended the same conventions. However, we had a number of things in common, particularly our burning curiosity about occult matters, and this inspired us to keep in contact over the miles and over the years.

When I started to discuss dreamwalking with Casey, presenting my theories on the technique, he was intensely curious. His first question involved the kind of distance I could travel. The vast majority of my dreamwalking excursions up to that point had been limited to friends in my home state of Ohio, although I had been able to verify at least two instances of dreamwalking to a friend in Milwaukee, Wisconsin. That was a distance of about 430 miles. I mentioned that another friend had gone to England for college, and I had attempted roughly the same experiment with her. England, for whatever reason, seemed beyond my reach. Considering the distance involved in that jaunt, neither of us had been surprised.

Casey's next question was whether or not I thought I could dreamwalk to him. At this point, we had exchanged energy on a number of occasions, and beyond the connections inevitably formed by this, we definitely had a bond of close friendship.

"Sure," I said. "Why not?"

And so began a series of experiments that would ultimately raise some serious questions about what was going on when I dreamwalked.

A MATTER OF TIMING

I can't say that our experiment was flawlessly scientific, but we did our best to maintain a certain amount of objectivity. The agreement was this: Casey knew to expect me any time after a certain date. From that point forward, we would both keep records of our dreams. I would record the time and date of each time I intentionally dreamwalked to him. He, for his part, would make note of when he felt contact, and he usually followed this up with a phone call for verification the next day. We would compare details over the phone, thereby verifying that we were in fact sharing the same dream as opposed to him simply having me appear as a character in an ordinary dream. The shared elements of the dreams were key, because we knew that even though he did not know which specific nights he should expect me, he would nevertheless have me on his mind. Dream content is in part influenced by what we've been thinking about during the day, and so there was a strong likelihood that I would appear in Casey's regular dreams simply because he was thinking about our experiment.

There is a three-hour time difference between Ohio and California. This fact caused a little confusion in some of our initial contacts, because some of the times were not matching up. Once we sorted the issue out, we laughed at ourselves for overlooking such a key detail, joking about how really smart people are often distinctly lacking in common sense. Our inability to keep track of time, however, brought the experiment to a screeching halt one fateful night.

I usually mixed up the times of my contacts so Casey would not learn to expect my arrival at any specific point in the night. On this particular occasion, I finished with work sooner than expected, and so I started a dreamwalking session fairly early in the night. I put a little soft music on, lit some incense, turned off the lights, and lay back in my bed. I entered the hypnagogic state without much difficulty, and from there transferred immediately to what seemed to be a cluttered room. The lights were on. There was laundry on the floor, and I remembered some comic poster on the wall. I thought it might have been the Green Lantern, but I didn't trust that impression simply because I knew Casey had a fondness for that character and nearly always wore a silver Green Lantern ring he had had made.

I became aware of Casey in the "dream." He was sitting on the bed in this room. I tried to speak to him, but the dreamwalk ended very abruptly. I found myself slammed back to full consciousness in my own bed, all sense of being elsewhere immediately dispelled. I thought that I had perhaps come too awake and slipped out of the hypnagogic state. I tried relaxing and entering the dreamspace again, but I could not recapture the connection. I attempted to dreamwalk to Casey several times right after that, only to meet with frustration. It seriously felt as if something was blocking me and, puzzled deeply by the experience, I gave up for the night.

Casey called the next day.

"You were in my room!" he cried. His voice hovered somewhere between excitement and panic.

"You're right," I responded. "I dreamwalked to you last night."

"No," Casey corrected. "You were *in my room*."

It took a few moments for me to process this. I had never equated dreamwalking with astral projection. I had read about astral projection for years, but every time I had tried it, I had met with failure. I had never had any success with separating a second body from my body, a process that seemed integral to astral projection as it was described in every book I owned on the subject.

"Dude, you need to clean or something," I joked. "That place is a mess."

"The experiments are over," Casey replied, unamused.

"What?"

"You don't understand," Casey said. "I wasn't asleep. You just showed up in my room." On the other end of the phone, I heard him let loose a shaky breath. "Don't do that again. You scared me half to death."

And that was that. Casey had been sitting up in bed reading when I tried to dreamwalk to him. Failing to make contact in a dream, but nevertheless focused on him, I apparently manifested in the doorway and walked into his room. When Casey felt an unexpected entity enter his private space, his reaction was instinctive. A trained magickal worker, he threw up shields, effectively jettisoning me from the space. Even though he recognized me as the entity, he was still so shaken by the experience that he threw up additional wards and shielding throughout the room. His room was his personal inner sanctum, and even though I was partly invited, it felt like an intrusion. My subsequent attempts to walk to him for the rest of that night were met with failure because he was consciously protecting the room.

I never did get Casey to clarify whether or not he *physically* saw me walk into his room. He may have simply gotten a sense of my presence and recognized the energy signature, like he did with ghosts. I knew he could sense ghosts from the time that he'd visited my childhood home, which had always been haunted. Without my prompting, he had sensed the presence of the spirits and described a number of them to me. Considering that it was his ability to sense and describe energy bodies that drew him to me, such related skills came as no surprise.

Whether I had physically manifested or not, I had obviously seemed enough like a ghost to really freak him out, because I was unable to convince him to try things again. But I did learn some valuable lessons from this short-lived experiment. First, dreamwalking to someone across the Continental US felt the same as dreamwalking to someone right down the road. We had wondered whether or not there would be a time delay between sending and receiving to reflect some kind of travel. As far as we could tell by comparing our experiences, there was not. Once contact was made, if there was any travel really involved, it was instantaneous. A secondary concern with the distance was whether or not it would reduce the strength of the phenomenon. This also proved to not be the case. Physical distance, it seemed, had very little impact on dreamwalking.

The third thing we learned, quite unintentionally, was that dreamwalking might have far more in common with astral travel than I had ever suspected. At least, I had no other way at the time to explain how I showed up in Casey's room when I thought I was traveling into his dream. I had never experienced a sense of separating a second body and projecting it *outside* when I dreamwalked. Nevertheless, Casey perceived a second, nonphysical "me" in his room. It certainly *sounded* like I had unconsciously projected an astral body. Was that even possible?

Both dreamwalking and astral projection can loosely be classified as out-of-body techniques. Although both techniques seek to project a portion of the self beyond the self, there are significant details that separate the two. Astral projection seeks to detach a second, etheric body and send this outward to explore the physical world from the vantage point of spirit as well as to travel beyond, to the further reaches of the astral planes. While individual experiences of astral projection can vary greatly, these two details—the projection of a second body and the sense of outward travel—remain constant. Dreamwalking, on the other hand, starts off in a mental space, traveling inward to reach its goal. Although the dreamwalker reaches out to specific people, dreamwalking "travel" occurs in the dreamspace, an internal realm that is connected, mind to mind.

If dreamwalking simply takes us along the pathways of dream, never venturing out into the physical world, how can we explain Casey's experience? The answer may lie in yet another out-of-body technique that moves inward, along the pathways of dream, in order to travel outward to this as well as other worlds. That technique is known as shamanism.

SHAMAN DREAMS

Shamanism allows trained individuals to harness certain trance states and travel to alternate realities. Interestingly, these alternate shamanic worlds are sometimes collectively referred to as "the dreamtime." The relation between this term and the "ancestor dreamings," or *altjiranga mitjinai*, of the Australian aborigines is clear and direct. They are both intended to refer to a mythic landscape that is at once an internal vision but also an external reality. The practices of the Australian aborigines are shamanic in nature, and their tradition has influenced a number of modern shamans.

With another fourth-grader teaching me how to dreamwalk, lucid dream, and achieve vision states, it should come as no surprise that one of the first magickal systems I studied as I grew up was shamanism. In shamanism I found a wealth of parallels with the things Pearl talked about, as well as with my own personal experiences.

Michael Harner's classic work, *The Way of the Shaman*, teaches experiential shamanism based on practices Harner himself was exposed to during a trip through the Amazon Basin. Through repetitive drumming or other techniques, the shaman enters an altered state of consciousness. In this visionary state, the shaman enters the "dreamtime" or shamanic reality. Like the dreamtime of the aborigines, this shamanic dreamtime is at once a realm of dreams and myths, but also a gateway to other realities. This concept of the Gates of Dream should be familiar by now.

In shamanic practice, the actual process of transition is often achieved by climbing into a cave or diving to the bottom of a lake while in the vision. Mircea Eliade, who wrote a much more academic treatise called *Shamanism: Archaic Techniques of Ecstasy*, also tells us that some shamans actually climb a pole in an attempt to physically act out this internal transition. The pole represents the *axis mundi*, or World Tree — the point of connection between the worlds.

There are many different symbols by which this process of transition manifests. The important thing, at least to our current studies, is that the transition is often an *inward* one. The shaman travels into himself in order to come out the other side. This aspect of the shamanic journey is one reason why shamanic practices have been so easily integrated into the Western New Age movement and other modern magickal practices. Shamanic journeying dovetails very neatly with Jungian psychology. The shamanic dreamtime, as a realm of myths and images that is peopled by animal totems and celestial teachers, can very easily be equated to Jung's collective unconscious, the psychological repository of humanity's collective myths, dreams, and symbols. Many of the totems and other mythic figures encountered in the shamanic realms are Jungian archetypes transported from their existence as simple concepts to vivid, potent entities.

These concepts also lead us directly back to the beliefs of the ancient world, where the realm of dreams was considered to be a kind of gateway to other levels of existence. While some dreams were certainly just images conjured by the mind, the realm of dreams could connect to another space, allowing gods to contact mortals from their eternal realms, and occasionally allowing mortals to travel forth and walk the realms of the gods.

This is the key to dreamwalking. There is a kind of travel that occurs in dreamwalking, but it is, at first, an inward journey. This inward journey, however, can lead the dreamwalker elsewhere. Traveling within can sometimes lead you out.

SHAPERS AND DREAMERS

The main goal of dreamwalking is to simply descend into one's own dreamspace, and then cross the boundaries between that and the dreams of another. This realm of dreams is at once subjectively symbolic and objectively real. It is a landscape touched upon by the shamanic dream-time and Jung's collective unconscious, and it is a landscape that starts in the core of each person's mind. Its deepest levels, as Jung himself observed, connect us all in mysterious ways. A dreamwalker harnesses this connection, using the paths that connect our dreams and imaginations in order to navigate the territory from one mind to another.

This is a function of mind that is much deeper than telepathy. On one level, the territory a dreamwalker proposes to traverse is merely a creation of the mind. And yet, as the ancients have noted, it acts like a place, and it should therefore be treated like a place. It is an *alam almithral*, a world of images, created by the mind but nevertheless, on some level, real.

Whether or not you accept that the dreamspace is an objective place that exists on some level unto itself, it still *works* that way. By descending into the realm of dreams, the dreamwalker travels inward, to travel out. Most considerations of space, and even many of the issues that astral travelers encounter in the energetic echo of the physical world, are circumvented. Does this mean that a dreamwalker can use this internal doorway to travel into the outside world? From my experience with Casey, and other, later experiments, I would have to say yes.

Although a dreamwalker aims for the dreamspace, sometimes the connection with the target elides into another sort of contact. If the target person is awake, the dreamwalk is much more likely to turn into a more familiar instance of astral projection. If the target is not present in dreams, then it's only natural for the dreamwalker to seek the target in person. Since inward journeys to the realm of dream can allow access to other levels of reality, there is little difficulty transitioning from the dreamspace to the subtle reality. These nonphysical places are all connected in intricate ways, and these complex interconnections are a major reason why any technique that attempts to move beyond physical reality can manifest in a myriad of forms. The Gates of Dream open many doors. It's not always easy to predict which one you're walking through.

CHAPTER FOUR

PREPARING THE WAY

WHEN YOU ARE GOING TO RUN A MARATHON, you don't just go into it cold. A lot of work and preparation goes into toning your body and building your endurance so that, when the time comes, you are up to the task. If you are reading this book, I think it's safe to assume that you are not the magickal equivalent of a couch potato. You probably know at least a little about energy work and meditation. You probably perform some kind of magick or ritual now and again. Dreamwalking is hardly as demanding as a marathon, but it's not a technique you should jump into cold.

Before you undertake the work of dreamwalking, you should take some time to prepare. The ideal preparation will involve not only preparing yourself for the work but also preparing your space for the work. In chapter two, we laid some groundwork that will prepare you internally for the experience ahead. All of the preparations covered in this chapter are intended to produce the most ideal environment possible for you to undertake your first few forays into the dreamspace.

Keep in mind that you do not have to perform these exercises precisely as they are written. The actual symbols and even many of the actions in the following exercises are not what's important. The important part of these preliminary exercises is the energetic work beneath the symbols and actions, and the mental state that that work is intended to inspire. If you find that certain images or visualizations do not appeal to you, feel free to substitute things that do. As we have covered elsewhere in this book, there are as many ways to perform most magickal techniques as there are people who perform them. As long as you retain the concept and the fundamental mechanics, you can innovate till to your heart's content.

BUILDING A DREAMING CHAMBER

When I am doing intense dreamwork, I always want to feel as safe and secure as possible. Some practitioners of astral projection seem to feel that they become so detached from their physical bodies that those bodies become vulnerable and could easily come to harm. Dion Fortune and others state very clearly that the body of someone engaged in any out-of-body travel should be in a safe, secure place, possibly even watched over by others.

This is not precisely the case with dreamwalking, at least not for me. Even when I dreamwalk from a full sleep state, I nevertheless will wake if someone enters my room or if there is some significant disturbance in my home. When I am dreamwalking from a borderline state, such as the hypnagogic state, my sensitivity to my physical surroundings is actually heightened, so that I will zero in on any little sound or movement in the general area, attempting to identify its nature and source and assessing its relevance to me.

In many ways, it is this hypersensitivity that creates the need for a dreaming chamber. A dreaming chamber is simply a safe space that is quiet and undisturbed where you can pursue your dreamwork. The ideal space will be psychologically and energetically conducive to the work you want to pursue. It will be clear and uncluttered, both physically and energetically, and it will be free from the possibility of intrusions. Creating a dreaming chamber is a fairly simple matter, and most people will be able to turn their bedrooms into functional dreaming chambers with only minimal effort.

The basic qualities you want to achieve are:
- An open space, clear of clutter
- A quiet space where you can reduce disturbances
- A space free from electronic devices
- A dark space you can protect from light
- A space that is comfortable, both physically and mentally

First, a dreaming chamber should be as simple and as uncluttered as possible. Most people will be working from their bedrooms, and for many of us, reducing clutter in our living spaces is a constant uphill battle. However, do not slack on the issue of clutter and space if you intend to turn your bedroom into an ideal dreaming chamber. By the principles of Feng Shui, physical clutter in a room affects the energy flow in that room. Also, clutter in a room can have a psychological impact on people who spend time in that room. Subconsciously, clutter is chaotic and distracting, and it can be harder to concentrate in a room where, everywhere you turn, you are reminded of laundry that needs doing, books that need shelving, and papers that need filing.

So you want a space that is clean and clear, someplace where you can be at peace in mind as well as in body. In addition to removing clutter, you want to reduce the number of potential distractions in this place. You want a room that is as quiet as possible, someplace that you can close off from intruding family members or nosy household pets. Some pets are actually a helpful addition to a good dreaming chamber. My cat Katya, for example, will stand guard for me when I go dreaming. She's a good little guardian because she hunkers down on the trunk at the foot of my bed, and she knows not to climb on the bed or poke at me while I'm off traveling through the dreamspace. The only time she broke this rule was when I needed to wake up and pay attention to something going on in the other room.

If you have a pet who is as attuned to your needs and as respectful of magickal work as Katya, there is obviously no need to exclude this companion from your dreaming chamber. However, if you happen to have one of those family dogs who just doesn't understand that he shouldn't jump up on the bed and slobber all over you while you're dreaming, you should consider effective ways to keep him out. Cats that are a little too self-focused to care whether or not you're busy are also potential distractions you will want to keep out. Nothing will pull you out of a nice, deep dreaming state like a damp toy mouse dumped unceremoniously on your face because Kitty wants to play.

Unless you live out in the middle of nowhere, it can be nearly impossible to insure that your dreaming chamber is completely free of extraneous noise. Even if you don't live with other people, few homes are spaced far enough apart to prevent noise from passing from one to another. One way to combat this is to have a white noise generator set up in your room. A small fan, set on a medium setting, will produce enough white noise to drown out most other distracting sounds. Soft music that can just blend into the background will work as well. Whatever route you take to help drown out distracting noises, you want to place any electronic item as far away from your bed as possible so the machine does not interfere with the flow of energy.

Televisions, computers, and a great many other electronic devices produce a low-level electric whine, even in sleep mode. According to most practitioners of Feng Shui, you shouldn't even keep electronic devices in the room you sleep in because the radiation they produce can have a negative impact on that room's energy. However, for a variety of reasons, it can be very difficult to keep your room completely appliance-free. At the very least, you need a clock and a lamp, and possibly a white noise generator. If you were to follow the strictest principles of Feng Shui, even these important devices could bring too much electronic pollution into your sleeping space.

When space and modern needs are considerations, how does one reduce the impact electronic devices have on a dreaming chamber? First, try to keep the big devices, such as computers and televisions, as far away from your bed as possible. For a very long time, I had a computer in my room, but I separated it from my bed first by a curtain and later by a screen. A small room divider set up between the foot of the bed and any computer desk can help to block a lot of the disruptive energy that many energy workers feel emanates from electronic devices. Turning computers completely off before you lay down to do any dreamwork is also helpful, as is unplugging any electronic devices that are not completely essential. If you can get things down to just one lamp, something to play music, and a clock, you'll be doing good. Practitioners of Feng Shui would also suggest that you try to keep the actual wires to electronic devices as far away from your bed as possible. I've found that this certainly doesn't hurt.

Not everyone is so energetically sensitive that devices like this cause them trouble. Some people even seem to thrive on the electric buzz of technological gadgets. As with everything else, consider the suggestions, but decide what works best for you.

As you refine the physical space of your dreaming chamber, you will also want to consider the placement of your bed. I have found that a central location works best. Don't push the side of your bed up against one wall or another: you want open space on either side of you as you perform your dreamwork. The idea is for you to feel as free and unrestricted as possible when you lie down to do your dreamwork. To this end, you may also want to consider moving the head of your bed at least a foot away from any wall. If you have a bed with a headboard, this could be irrelevant. Personally, I have neither a headboard nor a footboard on my bed so as to encourage the most open sensation possible. Remember: dreamwalking is a form of nonphysical travel, and you want an environment that promotes a sense of freedom to help you get past the barriers of your body.

Light can be an issue for many people when they are attempting out-of-body travel of any sort. It's no coincidence that the vast majority of experiments reported by seasoned astral projectors like Sylvan Muldoon and Robert Monroe occurred at night. Just as the dim electric whine of a computer in sleep mode can be a distraction, putting small amounts of radiation into the room, light also can be a distraction as we tune our senses to a more refined level of perception. We often forget that light itself is a form of radiation, and if part of the state we enter in order to dreamwalk involves a heightening of our energetic senses, then it only makes sense that we can become hypersensitive to light.

I prefer to have my dreaming chamber in a windowless room. Currently, it is underground, in my basement, so it is as insulated from light, sound, and other intrusions as possible. However, when I had a bedroom on the second floor of an apartment building, there was no place to put my bed but against a wide window that stretched nearly the length of one wall. To cover this, I used a double-thickness of cloth. Black-out fabric can be purchased as well—it's relatively inexpensive and just about any fabric store will carry it. In the house where I grew up, my grandmother would cut a sheet of cardboard and put this in the window, partly to help insulate the room in the winter, but it was very effective at keeping out the light.

The final consideration for constructing an ideal dreaming chamber is an aesthetic one. People tend to feel most comfortable in places that they find aesthetically pleasing. The décor and layout of a room can also help to contribute to the expressed purpose of that room. While your particular aesthetics are likely to be as unique as your fingerprints, there are a couple of guidelines that you can work from:

APPEAL TO ALL OF YOUR SENSES

As you build the aesthetic aspect of this space, don't overlook any of your five senses. You want a place that is visually appealing, and you want decorations that remind you that this is a special space, set apart from the mundane world. However, don't just stop with the overall look of the room. Put on some quiet music. Add candles and incense. If you have no great love for incense, try keeping fresh flowers in the room, or pick out an air freshener that just screams "dreaming chamber" to you. Consider the sheets and blankets you have on the bed. Are they comfortable? Do they appeal to you on a tactile level? You might want to consider going out and buying a special blanket and laying this out on the bed each time you dreamwalk.

CREATE A SPECIAL SPACE

A dreaming chamber is, by nature, a little exotic. It's more than just a bedroom. It's a ritual chamber. The way you decorate this room should remind you of the otherworldly quality of the work you will be doing here. Pick out a piece of art that inspires a dreamlike state when you look at it, and place this over your bed. Find the statue of a god or other mythic figure who has potent connections to the realm of dreams. Select colors, objects, and other decorations that evoke a dreamlike mood. My dreaming chamber has rich purple draperies hanging from the walls. The effect is stunning, and it was remarkably inexpensive to achieve. Check the bargain bins at your local fabric store for silky or sheer bolts of cloth in a color that you like. Get creative and transform this room from something ordinary to a space that transports you to another world the moment you walk through the door.

Once you have set up the ideal physical space, then you're ready to take your dreaming chamber to a whole new level: building the chamber's energy.

CREATING THE LOTUS OF THE DREAMER

To begin building your chamber's energy, sit on the floor in the exact middle of the room. If this is not possible, sit in the space closest to the middle. Sit with your back straight and your hips rocked forward ever so slightly. Place your hands on your knees and let your arms hang loosely against your sides. Close your eyes and let your head drop toward your chest. Press your tongue against the roof of your mouth and breathe slowly and evenly through your nose. If you have persistent allergies like me, taking some kind of allergy medicine about thirty minutes before you attempt this exercise makes things go much more smoothly!

Take several minutes to just sit in this posture and breathe. Let yourself get comfortable, and feel that inner point of relaxation begin to come into focus. As you concentrate on breathing, you may begin to have random, unwanted thoughts emerge in your mind: anxieties about your workday; concerns about money or cleaning the house; worries about whether or not you can succeed at this exercise. Don't fight them when they come, but don't focus on them either. Just acknowledge that these are your thoughts and let them pass right through you.

When the inner distractions have slowed down and you feel a warm, comforting hum begin to vibrate through your limbs, you are ready to begin. As you breathe, begin to build a sphere of energy within you, holding it in your belly so the bottom part of it rests almost on the tops of your thighs. Build this sphere a little more each time you inhale, seeing the sphere grow brighter with each intake of breath. As you concentrate on building the sphere of energy, think about what you want to achieve with your dreaming chamber. Think about your purpose, your long-term goals. Think about how you want the chamber to feel. Think about being safe in your dreaming chamber, but also able to reach out and perceive things over great distances.

With each new thought and desire, add another layer onto this glowing sphere of energy. Imbue that sphere with everything you seek to achieve with this room in regard to dreamwalking. When you are happy with what you have built up inside of you, turn your attention to the foundation of the room. First, feel the floor beneath you. Feel how your body is supported by that floor. Feel it with every inch of you that is resting upon the floor, in the middle of the room. Allow the sphere of energy to drop down past your thighs until it, too, is in contact with the floor.

This part of the set-up process will go more smoothly if you are setting up a dreaming chamber on a ground floor or in a basement. The connection to earth will facilitate this connection to the foundation of your chamber. If you are on a second or third floor, you may find yourself becoming suddenly aware of the fact that there is only a thin layer of wood and plaster between you and the room below you. In this case, what you are going to have to do is make a conscious choice to set your room apart from the other spaces around it. See a clear separation between the room you are working in and any other living space that happens to be below it. Once you can block out all the other floors between you and the ground, take a few moments to concentrate only on the ground itself. Imagine that where your body meets the floor, a thick, stable, stone pillar descends straight down into the earth. This pillar connects your room to the ground, holding it up like the sturdy, elegant stem of some exotic flower. Like that stem, this pillar should also allow energy to pass up from the earth to nourish what you are building. Waste energy will flow down the pillar into the ground; fresh, clean energy will pass back up. Even if you are on a ground floor or in a basement, you don't want to overlook this part. Make a connection to earth and concentrate on having that connection establish a flow of energy.

When you have established the connection to earth, thereby setting the "roots" of your dreaming chamber, turn your attention to the room itself. With your eyes still closed, picture the room around you clearly in your mind's eye. See it from every angle as it stretches out around you. Take a few moments to examine the room with your inner vision, seeing it in as much detail as possible. Do not limit yourself to just one perspective, but imagine the room as it would appear to an eye capable of seeing with 360-degrees vision. Do not lose your focus on the sphere of energy, nor your connection to the ground, as you are doing this.

Once you have a complete image of the room around you fixed in your mind's eye, send the energy you have gathered down into the floor—but be careful not to send it straight down into the ground! Instead, allow it to seep out of you where you are touching the floor, spreading out around you like a glowing pool of energy. Let the energy spread through the floor two feet on either side of you, then three feet, then four. See the energy ripple as it spreads, reaching for the base of the walls. When it reaches the walls, keep sending energy out from the sphere you have gathered inside of you. If you feel as if you are running out, pull upon the pillar and draw more energy up from the ground.

Envision the energy making contact with the walls and then flowing up them. With you as the center, see the energy spread to every corner of the room, flowing up and up until it reaches the ceiling, and then flowing inward across the ceiling. As you extend this energy through the room, keep in mind that you are establishing your boundaries. Nothing can get in that you don't want to enter, but the energy will allow you free passage. This is important because you want to feel secure in this space. The area between these walls should be an automatic comfort zone, a place that you can enter and feel not only immediately relaxed but also immediately in touch with more than physical reality.

If you build this right, the effects can be potent. You may find that this space begins to feel as if it occupies an entirely different realm than the rest of the building that it's in. When you walk through the door to this chamber and close it behind you, you may literally feel as if you have entered another world. You may also find that outside noises seem unnaturally muffled, as if the ordinary world beyond your walls simply cannot penetrate into the magickal space you have established.

Before the energy completely closes off the ceiling, take a moment to turn your attention inward, while at the same time not losing your mental grip on either the pillar beneath you or the rippling, fluid energy that has infused every corner of the room around you. Just as you felt your connection to earth and built a pillar going down to support and sustain your dreaming chamber, now you must reach up to the heavens with a thin line of pure energy—a glowing light the color of star-stuff works for me. This line of energy is gossamer thin, but so tensile and strong that nothing can break it. Send it up, straight out of the top of your head, and literally reach for the stars with it. For a moment, you will feel as if you are caught on a pin that reaches all the way up to the heavens and descends all the way into the earth. Don't let this feel uncomfortable. If you are Pagan or regularly work with some god or goddess, you can envision this line ending at that higher power. If, like myself, you do not work with godforms, simply feel the

connection to everything—you don't need to believe in a god or goddess to acknowledge that you are a part of something much bigger than
yourself. This golden thread is your line of expansion, a point that connects from the microcosm of you to the macrocosm of everything else.

Once you have built this thread clearly in your mind, allow the
energy you have been holding around a hole in the ceiling flow
around it. Do not seal the energy completely shut; the whole point of
your dreaming chamber is to build an energetic space that protects
you, but also provides easy passage in and out. This golden thread is
the point that holds open the door, and with its connection to Above,
it can be as big or as small as you need it to be.

At this point, you are nearly done building the energetic form of
your dreaming chamber. You have taken the energy you built up
inside of yourself and extended it out to the room, enforcing the floor,
the ceiling, and the walls. Every corner and nook of the room is
invested with this rippling, living energy, and you have established a
connection both Above and Below. The pillar you have sunk into the
earth is set to hold the chamber up, and it also passes energy up and
down, clearing anything unwanted that might build up over time, and
introducing new, fresh energy as it is need. The energy flowing from
you through the floor, ceiling, and walls is still raw, fresh, and rippling.
Although you have invested it with all your needs and desires for the
purpose of this room, it still has no fixed shape. Now you want to make
it permanent.

I have likened the pillar beneath you to a stem. The energy flowing
around you is supported by this stem, and it curves up, almost—but
not quite—closing over your head. The room around you is probably
rectangular, made of angles and planes. Energy does not easily flow at
right angles to itself. Although you imagined the energy spreading out
from you and climbing up the walls, then spreading out across the
ceiling, holding the energy at those severe right angles will not be easy.
To promote a natural flow to the energy you have invested in this
room, you want to allow it to curve around you, expanding slightly

beyond the physical shape of the room. To help with this process, you want to imagine a final shape to the energy, something that will allow for the easiest and healthiest flow possible.

You can imagine the energy around you taking the form of a glowing sphere, so long as you remember to allow for a small aperture at the top so you can pass freely in and out. Because we are delving into the realm of dreams, however, you may want a more mythically potent shape to the energetic structure of your dreaming chamber: a lotus flower. In the myths of ancient India, there is a story of a god who is dreaming. The dream of this god is the Universe, and it emerges from his sleeping form in the shape of a lotus flower. When he wakes, this particular version of the Universe ends, only for another to emerge in dreams when he falls back asleep. Seated in the lotus flower is the Lord of this Universe, who has the power to shape the dream.

By shaping the energy of your room roughly into the form of a lotus, you evoke this imagery. You become the Lord of the Universe, seated in the lotus flower, shaping the dream. If we accept that we are all connected on some level of myth, dream, and imagination, then even if you have no background whatsoever in the Hindu tradition from which this story comes, you will nevertheless draw upon thousands of years of meaning.

PREPARING YOURSELF

From a very physical standpoint, there are a few things you should consider prior to undertaking a dreamwalk. Some of these are common sense practices for any kind of demanding work—whether physical or spiritual—but I want to go over them just in case.

BE WELL-RESTED:

It may seem a little strange to ask that you feel well rested prior to attempting an exercise that may involve you falling asleep. There are two main reasons for this, however. First, some of the most successful methods for dreamwalking don't involve you actually going to sleep. Instead, they require that you hover in a borderline state between waking and sleep. If you are well-rested, it is much easier to maintain this state without being tempted to simply nod off. Secondly, even if you are planning on using a technique that harnesses lucid dreaming to launch you into dreamwalking, you still want to be rested and in good health. When we are exhausted, we tend to sleep very heavily. The more worn-out you are prior to going to sleep, the less likely you are to achieve the lucidity to control or even remember your dreams.

AVOID ARTIFICIAL STIMULANTS:

It should probably be a no-brainer, but avoid the intake of any artificial stimulants for at least three hours prior to dreamwalking. This means no caffeine and no nicotine, not to mention a number of other things that you probably shouldn't legally be taking anyway. Before you pout, there's good reason for this. Just as being too tired will negatively impact your performance in dreamwalking, being too wired will also affect how things work. You need to be able to relax very deeply in order to effectively harness the borderline state. You will create much more work for yourself than necessary if you try to make yourself relax with four cups of espresso vibrating through your veins. If you are on any medications, whether prescribed or over-the-counter, you should take a good look at their warnings as well. If at all possible, you should avoid any excessive stimulants or depressants prior to undertaking this work. Some substances, like the herbal substance melatonin, can also have an impact on the nature and intensity of your dreams. Consider these effects and their potential impact upon your work before taking anything.

EAT LIGHT, EAT EARLY:

You don't have to fast for an entire day prior to dreamwalking, but it's a good idea to take a little more care in what you eat in the twenty-four hours leading up to your work. Heavy, greasy, complicated meals should be avoided. Although you don't have to concentrate on it consciously, digestion takes up a lot of your body's resources. Those resources are better diverted to the work you want to do. And I don't know about anyone else, but I find belly gurgles exceptionally distracting.

Once you have the issue of physical preparation out of the way, it's time to turn your mind to preparations of a more spiritual nature. If you are an old pro at magickal workings, then you probably already have a set routine for how you get into the right frame of mind before you attempt a technique. But if you're just starting out, there are a couple of things you should do to get yourself into the "zone" before you attempt an actual magickal working.

The very first thing is grounding and centering. This is a simple exercise that eventually will become second nature. The idea behind the exercise is to flush your energy of anything hurtful or distracting, and then to rebalance yourself so you can start from a calm and focused center.

There are a number of ways to ground and center. For the most part, the only real difference between all the various techniques involves imagery. When we work with energy, our own or someone else's, it helps to visualize what we want to accomplish. Visualization is sometimes mistaken for fantasy, but although it is also an exercise of imagination, visualization is a technique that puts your imagination to work. The imaginative part of visualization simply involves picking a series of images that have symbolic meaning for you that then work as cues to your subconscious mind to accomplish something you can't really tell it in words. As we've covered elsewhere in this book, all the deeper parts of your mind communicate in images and symbols. In order to get your whole brain focused on a task, then, you need to speak in a language that all the different parts of your head understand. That universal language is symbol, although precisely which symbol set equates to the universal language of your brain will vary widely from person to person, which brings us back to why there are so many different techniques out there for grounding and centering. The actual mechanics of the technique remain the same regardless of what imagery they're couched in. Before we go over a sample visualization, it will be helpful to directly address those mechanics.

First, let's look at grounding. Grounding magickally works on the same principle as grounding a wire. Energy is going to pass through your body as you perform your magickal working. To a certain extent, you have energy passing in and out of you constantly, every day. But when you consciously work what we call magick, then the amount of energy and its intensity is heightened significantly. In the physical world, when you pass too much energy through a wire, you can burn the wire out. Although you are not dealing with electricity, shunting too much energy through your system can also burn you out. Grounding connects you to the earth, providing a stabilizing principle that at once helps support your ability to channel energy and also provides a safe place for excess energy to go. Unwanted energy or energy that feels incompatible with you can be shunted from your system with grounding as well. Anything that compromises the health and stability of your system will pass out of you, into the ground.

If you do nothing else than imagine that you have an energetic connection to earth from which you draw stability and through which you pass off any energy that you find to be too much, then you are successfully grounding.

Centering is a matter of balance. Your entire body is wired for energy, with energy passing in and out and through you all the time. The very shape of your body, with its inherent symmetry, helps this process to have a certain balance to it. Energy is spread out across your system at all times, so there is energy in your head, energy in your feet, and energy moving in between. One slight problem with grounding is that it makes you focus a little more energy into your feet than you normally would. Your feet are the part of you that's touching earth almost all the time, and so it's only natural for there to be a greater focus on energy there, or in any other part of your body touching the ground, when you are consciously grounding.

To regain your balance once you consciously connect yourself to earth, you want to make an equal and opposite connection in the other direction—that is, *up*—and then find your own center in between. For some people, that center is in the middle of the chest, at the base of the sternum, or just a little lower. Others find that they naturally focus on a center in their belly, cradled in their hips. It's possible that your own center will be placed a little differently, but for the most part, the center will be located in the center of your body.

Centering is the act of reaching down and then up with your energy, and then seeking the balance that is in between. On a cognitive level, this helps you achieve a sense of mental balance as well, allowing you to occupy a comfortable middle zone between body and spirit.

One of the most common ways to visualize grounding and centering is to imagine that you are a tree. To ground, feel roots extending from your feet deep into the earth. The roots pass unwanted energy down, pulling fresh and vital energy back up. The roots also stabilize you, creating a firm foundation for you to stand upon. After you have established your roots, then raise your arms over your head and imagine that these extend into branches. Reach up and out to the sky with these branches just as you reached deep and down into the earth with your roots. Feel yourself stretching and spreading between these two points: earth and sky, Below and Above. Your connection to the sky raises your energy and makes it feel light and airy. Where earth grounds and stabilizes, sky reminds you to bend and flow.

When you can feel yourself balanced comfortably between these two points, take your hands and hold them over your center. Picture your center as a glowing sphere of energy. Cup it in your hands and fix the sensation of internal balance, stability, and flow, into this central point. When you have a clear sense of center and that comfortable balance echoes through mind, spirit, and body, let the image of the tree slowly fade away until you are just yourself again. You are a living, breathing person, but the balance remains.

From this balanced state, you may want to take another few minutes to prepare yourself for the work ahead. Think of this as the stretches you do before a work-out so you don't strain any muscles. Sit somewhere that's comfortable and take some time to just breathe. Don't let go of your sense of center. Instead, build from this center and let the calm, comfortable focus spread all throughout you. Breathe slowly in and out while you do this, and start thinking about what you want to accomplish with your dreamwalking. If you have made arrangements to visit a friend, call that person to mind. Think of what that person looks like. Recall the sound of that person's voice. Evoke your sense of that person's energy, scent, what emotions you feel when you're around this friend. If you have something that belongs to this person, hold the item in your hand and feel the energy still lingering on it. You might even consider specifically asking for an item you can focus on, some small object you can use as a touchstone when reaching out to this person.

If you are nervous about things, reassure yourself. Draw upon that balanced center and accept that you can achieve what you want, if you accept that it's possible. Don't allow worry or fear of failure to consume you. Focus instead on your strengths. Don't just remind yourself to be confident: feel confident. Tell yourself what you want, then tell yourself that you are going to succeed.

Sometimes I find it helps to solidify your intent if you say it out loud. In a lot of ways, I think this is why prayer appeals to so many people. It's not so much the idea that someone will hear your request, but that you openly state the request out loud. The ancient Egyptians, a favorite culture of mine, attributed a lot of power to words—so much, in fact, that to erase a person's name from written texts was to erase that person from reality. Countless creation myths, including the all-time bestseller of Western civilization, the Bible, begin with the Word. Psychologically this has validity as well. When you speak something out loud, you have to give it that extra bit of attention to focus it from an ambiguous and amorphous desire to something concrete enough *for* words. So—even if you feel silly doing it at first—I highly recommend taking a few moments to clearly state your intent out loud. Although, if your embarrassment to effect ratio is too high, then you can just try thinking it very clearly to yourself. For the best effect, try not to think in just feelings or images, but form each word very clearly in your mind.

> Tell yourself:
> I am the dreamer, and this is my dream.
> I am the dreamer, and this is my dream.
> I am the dreamer, and this is my dream.

Do you feel it as a reality within you? Do you believe it, all the way to the center of your being? Now you are ready to begin.

CHAPTER FIVE

OPENING THE GATES
OF DREAM

THERE ARE TWO TYPES OF DREAMWALKING: dreamwalking from the borderline state between waking and sleep, and dreamwalking from full sleep. Dreamwalking from the borderline state feels much more like meditation or creative visualization. The dreamwalker remains partially awake, consciously directing the action of the dream. Dreamwalking directly from the state of REM sleep is literally the ability to walk to other people while dreaming. This is classic dreamwalking, and it is at once easier and more difficult to learn than dreamwalking from the borderline state.

Most people have a natural capacity to dreamwalk. However, because it occurs when we sleep, dreamwalking is typically initiated and controlled by the unconscious mind. These spontaneous experiences of dreamwalking often arise as a response to personal crisis or need. One of the goals of this book is to help people become aware of this unconscious ability so they can begin to exercise it with conscious intent. To this end, the first type of dreamwalking we are going to address is classic dreamwalking. This is the type of dreamwalking that is most likely to occur spontaneously. In order to harness and direct this ability, we first need to learn how to achieve a greater degree of control over our dreams.

THE MECHANICS OF DREAMING

Classic dreamwalking typically occurs during full REM sleep. REM stands for "Rapid Eye Movement." This is the stage of sleep where the most vivid dreaming occurs and it is so named because our eyes visibly track dream images from behind our closed lids. Classical writer Lucretius remarked upon the phenomenon of Rapid Eye Movement as long ago as 50 B.C.E., and yet it wasn't until the 1950s, in a sleep laboratory in Chicago, Illinois, that modern science definitively linked Rapid Eye Movement with dreaming.

Many people have no recollection of dreaming, and yet we know that everyone enters REM sleep on average four times a night. Even blind people experience REM sleep, unless the muscles of their eyes have completely atrophied. We can tell that dreaming serves a crucial physiological function only by negation: deprived of REM sleep, people have trouble thinking clearly and will begin to experience visual and sometimes auditory hallucinations.

Thanks to developments such as the EEG or electroencephalogram, modern scientists can measure the changes in brain wave patterns experienced during sleep and dreams. From this, we can identify four distinct stages of sleep. On the edge between sleeping and waking, our brain waves move in patterns called alpha and theta waves. The theta waves are high amplitude, low frequency waves, which means that they are slow, but have very high peaks. In the next stage, those peaks begin to increase in patterns known as sleep spindles and the alpha waves drop off, until only theta waves remain. Both of these stages only last a few minutes each. Stage two, the theta waves accented with sleep spindles, gives way to deep sleep, otherwise known as delta sleep. Deep sleep is indicated by delta waves, which are very slow compared to alpha and theta waves. We go through two stages of deep sleep, one with mixed delta and theta waves, the other with more than fifty percent delta waves.

Dreaming does not occur directly from deep sleep. Instead, the stages quickly reverse themselves, and we emerge into REM sleep.

Our first stage of REM sleep lasts approximately ten minutes. When we dream, brain activity jumps, moving in high frequency beta waves, intermixed with the occasional theta wave. Beta waves are not exclusive to sleep; our brains produce beta wave activity when we are awake as well. A full series of these stages takes about ninety minutes to complete. The average person experiences four such series in a night, with the periods of deep sleep gradually waning and the periods of REM sleep increasing to as many as thirty minutes in length. The final period of REM sleep is not only the longest, it is also the one that lingers most clearly in memory as we emerge from sleep. Dreamwalking can occur in any of these stages of REM sleep.

THE MAN BEHIND THE CURTAIN

Dreamwalking from a full state of REM sleep may seem like a difficult prospect. The very act of going to sleep means relinquishing consciousness. Short of instances of lucid dreaming, there is no way to exert conscious control over our dreams. So how do we manage to consciously dreamwalk from a full sleeping state? Much of this comes down to learning how our conscious and unconscious minds communicate, then taking advantage of this communication.

Dreams are the province of the unconscious mind. As anyone who has interpreted the meaning of dreams knows, the unconscious speaks to us in the language of symbol and metaphor. In order to talk to our unconscious mind, it's necessary to approach it on the same level. This is the fundamental premise behind techniques like visualization and active imagination. Methods that consciously craft images with the imagination seek to send a message to our deeper selves, bridging the gap between conscious and unconscious. It is not the images themselves that have power but the meaning behind them. This meaning is encoded within the images, cuing our unconscious to help us achieve our desires.

It's important to remember that the unconscious mind makes up a larger portion of who we are than the more familiar conscious mind. The self we identify as "I" lives in the conscious portion of our minds, but most of what we experience every day comes from the unconscious. We already know that our dreams arise from this portion of our psyche, but so do our instincts and all the abilities that arise spontaneously, without conscious effort. The unconscious mind is the keeper of intuition and most psychic abilities, as well as vast portions of memory. If you think of your psyche as a house, your conscious mind is the living room, where you spend most of your time. Your unconscious mind is the basement and the attic and all of the many closets tucked away everywhere. These are the spaces where all of the machinery of the house is stored—the furnace and the water heater, the fuse box, and everything else that runs things behind the scenes. These are also the spaces where you store those things you want to keep, the things you can't bring yourself to throw away, and all the things you want to pretend aren't really there. While complete integration of the conscious and unconscious minds is neither likely nor advisable, cultivating a greater level of awareness and communication between the two has a number of benefits. Primary among these is gaining at least some measure of control over abilities that otherwise operate purely on instinct. Dreamwalking is one such ability.

When you built your dream haven in chapter two, it was not only intended to serve as a way-station between the waking world and the dreamspace. Your dream haven is also a halfway point between your conscious and unconscious minds. Crafted with symbols and images that have meaning to you, the very manner in which you constructed your dream haven, as well as your dream gate and your eidolon, were cues priming your unconscious to make these things real in the realm of dreams.

By the nature of consciousness, it is nearly impossible for the conscious mind to give direct orders to the unconscious. As much as we like to believe otherwise, it is the unconscious mind, not the conscious

"I," that is running the show. However, it is possible to give suggestions and place requests with the unconscious, and this is how we will learn to actively direct our dreamwalking from the state of full REM sleep.

PATHWAYS OF DREAM

The dream haven and dream gate visualizations, although helpful, are not strictly necessary for dreamwalking. They are convenient images that represent intent and meaning, communicating these to your unconscious mind. All of these exercises are about asserting your ability to control and direct events in the dreamspace, representing this intent with meaningful symbols so your unconscious will understand.

As helpful as such tools can be for communicating between conscious and unconscious, it's important to remember that they are tools only. Power does not come from a symbol; it comes from what that symbol represents.

The dream haven asserts that you have a presence in the dreamspace, and it helps acquaint you with how interaction occurs on this level of being. By consciously shaping your dream haven, you learn that you can exert control over this other space purely through the action of will. The very crafting of a dream haven is a clear statement to your unconscious that you can and will control the contents of the dreamspace. The mechanics behind shaping the dream haven can be applied directly to shaping other aspects of the dreamspace. The truth behind the symbol here is that, in the realm of dreams, imagination is king.

The dream gate represents a point of connection between you and other people in dreams. By crafting a dream gate, you tell your unconscious that, although the dream haven is your personal corner of the dreamspace, you are aware that there are other places out there, and you intend to be connected to them when you choose. This connection is established through the use of subtle links. Subtle links are strands of energy between people that are forged by emotional and energetic interactions of profound significance. These links are at work, for example, in the bond between mother and child, between lovers and close friends, or, as noted earlier, when friends finish each other's sentences. Siblings, and especially twins, often share a profound sort of subtle link, and this has even been the subject of a number of scientific experiments.

Sometimes we find that we have a tie to a perfect stranger, someone whom we've just met in this life, yet who seems like a friend we've known for ages. Because these links are subtle in nature, they do not go the way of mortal flesh. People we discover an immediate connection to are often familiar to us from previous lives. Psychiatrist Brian Weiss, author of *Many Lives, Many Masters*, believes that some souls choose to go through a cycle of lives together, connecting again and again as parents and children, lovers, and friends. All of these emotional bonds reinforce these links. The deeper the emotional connection, the deeper the link.

You can visualize these links a number of ways. A link can be seen as a tether that anchors you to your target, drawing your attention and your energy down to them. It can be like Ariadne's thread, leading you through the maze of reality until you arrive safely at your goal. It can be a path that connects your souls, a bridge of energy that each of you walk along freely. In dreamwalking, these links are best approached as the pathways of dream, for they are the anchor points that allow you to reach out to another person and connect in dreams. Your dream gate, in addition to representing the interconnectedness of all portions of the dreamspace, is a visible representation of these subtle links. When you call up the image of a person in your dream gate, what you are doing is pulling on the link. When you reach out and connect with the person, you are connecting energetically through the link.

In the exercise for classic dreamwalking that follows, you will start from your dream haven, using your dream gate as a focus for connection. However, I understand that certain visualizations may not work for everyone. While I encourage you to try the dream gate visualizations at least once, keep in mind what this image is meant to represent: the subtle connection between you and your target, and your ability to use this connection to reach out to them through the dreamspace. Knowing the fundamental meaning behind the symbol allows you to change that symbol until you hit upon a form that best conveys that meaning to you personally.

WALK THIS WAY

At this point, you have put a good deal of work into crafting the internal space of your dream haven. You've also put time and effort into crafting the external space of your dreaming chamber. If you are also well rested and in a good mental place, then we are ready to go. For each dreamwalk that you undertake, there are three main questions that you must answer:

- Who are you dreamwalking to?
- Why are you dreamwalking?
- What backdrop do you want for the dream?

For this first dreamwalking experience, we're going to keep things very simple. The purpose of this dreamwalk is simply to establish contact. The backdrop, or dream landscape, of this dreamwalk will be the area around your gate of dreams. As for who you are dreamwalking to, I will leave that decision up to you.

Enter your dreaming chamber and make yourself comfortable. You may want to light some incense, play some music, or turn on a white noise generator to make the space more conducive to the work ahead. Lay back, get comfortable, and focus on your target. Call this person to mind as clearly as possible. If you have an item that belongs to this person, you may wish to hold this in your hand or even place it under your pillow while you sleep. If you choose to use an item, it should be something that reminds you strongly of your target's energy, serving as an additional focus to help you connect. Another method of cuing your unconscious to target a specific person is to write out that person's name on a slip of paper. Read the name off of the slip of paper just before you lay down to begin, then place the paper under your pillow. This is a symbolic act that associates the name with sleeping and dreams. As simple as this trick may seem, it works.

Once you have established clear sense of your connection to the target, close your eyes and put yourself in your dream haven. Go to the area where you have erected your dream gate. Standing in front of your personal gate of dreams, focus on what you wish to accomplish with this dreamwalk. It may help for you to state your intent. In this case, you will simply say, "I wish to contact [Name]."

Once you have clearly established your intent, gaze into the gate of dreams, and call upon your connection to your target. Speak your target's name at least three times. You can state your target's name silently in your head, or you may speak it softly as you lay back in your dreaming chamber. Maintain your sense of the connection you share with this person throughout. As you focus on that connection, call up an image of your target in the gate of dreams. Focus upon this image until it seems as if your target is standing in front of you, just an arm's reach away. You may wish to reinforce your sense of connection to the target by reaching into the gate of dreams and laying your hand over their heart. Hold this image in your mind as you fall asleep. State your intent to connect with this person over and over again as you drift off.

IDENTIFYING SUCCESSES

When you wake up, write down the details of any dreams that you think might have been instances of successful contact. Don't get frustrated if your first few attempts at dreamwalking do not succeed. You will probably have to do this a number of times before you achieve any measure of success. Because you are dreamwalking from a full sleep state, you do not have absolute control over what happens once you fall asleep. The presleep visualization is your attempt to program your unconscious mind with your intent. Repeating your intent and repeating your target's name over and over again are a form of self-hypnosis. You are essentially programming what you want into your unconscious mind. While vivid and meaningful symbols are a way of translating your intent to your unconscious, repetition is a way of underscoring this intent. Similarly, repeating this exercise over a series of nights is more likely to yield a success.

It may also be difficult at first to measure a success. One of the problems with dreamwalking is that the person being dreamwalked to is far more likely to remember the experience than the person actually initiating the dreamwalk. As doctors Ullman and Krippner learned with their experiments in dream telepathy, a dreamer is far more likely to remember a dream in which foreign content is inserted into their dreamspace. As the person initiating the dreamwalk, there is nothing technically foreign in your dreamspace. In almost all intentional dreamwalks, you are reaching out to a person you already know and you have consciously crafted a dream landscape to your specifications. Since everything in this space is not only familiar to you but actually under your control, none of it is going to stand out as remarkable.

So how are you supposed to remember dreamwalking from full REM sleep? Again, repetition is the key. The more you dreamwalk, the more familiar you will become with how the experience feels. As the person initiating the dreamwalk, you may not have any conveniently remarkable material inserted into your dream to help you remember it in the morning, but dreamwalks are significantly different from ordinary dreams. If, when dreamwalking, you also keep a thorough record of your other dreams, you will begin to notice the hallmarks of a dreamwalk. If your dreaming partner also keeps a log, you can compare your suspected "hits" with theirs. This will give you an even greater opportunity to identify how dreamwalking manifests for you.

EXPANDING THE JOURNEY

Once you get the hang of just making contact in dreams, then you can begin to experiment with more elaborate journeys. In spontaneous cases of dreamwalking, a person typically responds to a personal crisis by instinctively reaching out to others in the dreamspace in order to communicate the nature of the crisis. However, dreamwalking can be used for much more than simply conveying messages in a crisis. Although dreamwalking takes place on the level of dreams, it nevertheless allows for interaction that feels as if it were happening face-to-face. This makes dreamwalking especially useful for people who find themselves separated by distances which they cannot overcome in the waking world. There are six main activities that can be carried out when dreamwalking intentionally:

- Communication
- Interaction
- Feeding and energy exchange
- Healing
- Instruction
- Spirit contact

There is a seventh activity that can be carried out in both intentional and unintentional cases of dreamwalking, which I've left off this list. Dreamwalking can also be used to carry out potent psychic attacks. I strongly discourage any such use of this technique. Since there are unethical people out there, however, we will go into methods of protecting yourself from such attacks in chapter nine.

COMMUNICATION:

We can use dreamwalking in order to convey important messages that we might not otherwise be able to deliver to a person in the waking world. I regularly create circumstances that are perfect for this application of dreamwalking. I have a tendency to get really focused on writing projects. When I get sucked into a project, I have a nasty habit of dropping out of contact for weeks or months at a time. I stop checking my e-mail, and I will sometimes go so far as to turn off my phone. Needless to say, this habit often alarms some of my friends—especially those who live far away from me. Once I have been out of contact for a few months and my friends are actively beginning to worry about me, a few of them have a standing invitation to drop by in the dreamspace and check up on me. Such a dreamwalk simply seeks to convey the question, "Are you okay?" I catch them up on what I'm doing (and if I'm really focused on the project, I ask them to stop bothering me!). When I finally get around to turning the phone back on, we verify the experience.

INTERACTION:

When it comes to dreamwalking, "interaction" is a fairly wide term. It covers a huge range of interpersonal relations, from simply hanging out with someone to a variety of a vicarious—and sometimes intimate—physical interactions. Meeting up with someone in the dreamspace simply to hang out may seem trivial at first. However, consider that in this day and age many people who live thousands of miles away from one another have been able to form profound friendships through the Internet. Although it is possible to cross that distance quickly and inexpensively through the mediums of e-mail and chat rooms, it is not always within someone's means to physically visit such a long-distance friend. Because dreamwalking can allow for interactions that feel as real as anything that takes place face-to-face, it can serve as a substitute for individuals who find themselves separated by great distance. Dreamwalking is not always as satisfying as physically being there with someone, but, given no other options, dreamwalking still allows for something significant to be shared.

FEEDING:

Ethical psychic vampires use dreamwalking in order to engage in energy exchange with willing partners. When a psychic vampire is isolated physically, or there are simply no willing donors nearby, dreamwalking is a workable solution. Psychic vampires certainly have the ability to feed over long distances, but long-distance feeding is typically inefficient, causing the psychic vampire to expend more energy than is gained through the effort. Dreamwalking circumvents this problem, allowing the psychic vampire to feed from a willing donor as if that activity were happening face-to-face.

HEALING:

Just as a psychic vampire can use dreamwalking to engage in energy exchange with a willing donor, so can an energy worker use dreamwalking to perform focused and efficient energy work on a long-distance target. This is especially useful for long-distance healing techniques, many of which function on the same principles as a psychic vampire's long-distance feeding techniques. By performing the healing in the dreamspace, many of the challenges that are usually associated with long-distance work are circumvented. A dreamwalker who performs healing techniques within the dreamspace can also harness the unique properties of that space to reinforce the healing with other applications of willwork, shaping the very landscape of dreams to be conducive to healing.

INSTRUCTION:

Individuals who use dreamwalking to communicate are often interested in conveying a simple message. Instruction differs from simple communication because it seeks to harness the dreamspace in order to teach. Dreamwalking most often occurs between only two people. However, it is in no way limited to this number of participants. It is possible to essentially use dreamwalking to teleconference, drawing a number of people into the same dreamspace where they can all interact with one another. This is a fairly advanced application of dreamwalking, but it is not impossible. This is especially useful for a teacher whose students live in many far-flung locations. Using the dreamspace for instruction also opens up a vast world of experiences and techniques. A skilled dreamwalker can specifically shape a dream landscape to instruct, creating situations that give students the equivalent of hands-on experience in a given technique.

SPIRIT CONTACT:

As we saw very early on in this book, interactions in the dreamspace are not limited purely to living people. The dreamspace can also be used to interact with the spirits of the dead. While it is far more common for the dead to contact us in the dreamspace, it is also possible for us to reach across the veil to someone we have a strong, lingering connection to. My only caution with this particular application of dreamwalking comes from the knowledge that sometimes spirits have better things to do than simply talk to those who they have left behind. Individuals who have recently died are far more likely to be reached through this method of communication. Spirits who have not worn mortal flesh for a year or more may very well have moved on to a different aspect of their journey. This is not to say that our departed loved ones forget us after a sufficient number of years. Quite the contrary, the ties that we establish with people in this life often linger over subsequent lifetimes. However, just as we have pressing needs and obligations in this life, spirits also have their business that they must attend to. Keep this in mind when seeking to reach out to someone who has passed physically out of your life.

If you wish to carry out any of these six main activities within the scope of your dreamwalk, you will have to expand your presleep visualization. Develop a clear statement of your intent, something you can boil down to just a few words. As you lay down and put yourself in your dream haven, repeat this intent over and over to yourself, programming it into your unconscious mind. Go to the area with your dream gate and call upon your connection with your target. Because your goal is more complex than simply reaching out and making contact with this person, take a few moments to imagine what form your intent should ultimately take. Consciously play this sequence of events out in your mind as you stand in front of your dream gate and focus on your connection to the target person. You may even want to consciously look through the dream gate and imagine that the sequence of events are playing themselves out just the way you want them to in the space beyond the gate. Put some effort into this visualization, envisioning each stage of interaction with your target person with both clarity and intent. Play the scenario over and over again as you fall asleep, never relinquishing the sense of your connection with your target.

As you work to make your dreamwalking experiences more involved, it is still best to stick with broad and simple themes.

If you are seeking to connect with a loved one to issue them a message in their dreams, the process is nearly identical. First, put the message in the simplest terms possible. Focus less on the words and more on their impact and meaning. Repeat the message to yourself several times until you feel that it's become firmly planted in your mind. When a message is the focal point of a dreamwalk, you may consider using the pillow technique for the message itself. Write the message out before retiring. Read it out loud to yourself while thinking clearly about your target. Then slip the message under your pillow and lay down to sleep.

As you lie back, think of a place where you will meet with your target. Imagine your target standing in that place. Imagine yourself standing in front of the person. Picture each word of the message in your mind, and imagine yourself speaking each of these words clearly to your target. Keep this entire exchange simple and direct, and repeat it several times before you fall asleep.

THE LANDSCAPES OF DREAM

As helpful as the dream haven and dream gate exercises can be, you do not always have to start a dreamwalk from these locations. Another way of elaborating on your dreamwalking journeys involves building more complicated and involved dream landscapes. As touched upon above, it is possible to tailor dream landscapes to specific instances of dreamwalking. If you dreamwalk into a pre-existing dream, you can impose your will upon your surroundings, building upon the already existing environment. You can also create a dream landscape from scratch, tailoring each aspect of the landscape to the overall intent of the dreamwalk.

You have had some practice with this technique already when you built your dream haven. Building any additional dream landscape will function exactly the same way. When you build a dream landscape you are under no obligation to make it a permanent abode. However, if you create a specific dream landscape for use with just one dreamwalking excursion, be certain to deconstruct the landscape once you are done, releasing the energy back into the dreamspace.

There is no specific danger inherent in creating and then abandoning a specific dream landscape, but don't be surprised if you find yourself stumbling upon these abandoned landscapes of dream during later trips into the dreamspace. Imbued with sufficient intent, a dream landscape can sometimes take on a life of its own, developing into an independent realm within the dreamspace. Sometimes, when we fantasize about an imaginary landscape, we do this unintentionally, creating an echo of that imaginary realm beyond the Gates of Dream. The dreamspace and the shamanic dreamtime verge upon the same territory, after all, and that territory includes not only the realm of dreams but also the realm of spirits and the realm of myths.

You can create a dream landscape any number of ways. You can write out a description of the desired location, crafting each detail with clear and concise words. You can draw a picture of the desired landscape, or you can find a pre-existing image you wish to reproduce. There are no limits to what you can do, so long as you engage your imagination and invest each detail with focused intent.

One of the easiest ways to shape a dream landscape is to simply state out loud what you want. If there is a particular place you want to find yourself in during the dreamwalk, name this place. If the desired location is some place that does not exist, then put together a simple yet thorough description. Repeat this description to yourself just before you fall asleep, building the image of the dream landscape in your mind just as you built your dream haven. When you are finished mentally building an image that conforms to your description, say out loud, "I will dreamwalk to [Name]. I will dreamwalk to this place." As you say this, clearly envision first the person, then the place. Then imagine the person standing in the desired location. Invest these images with focused intent, making them as real as possible in your mind.

If you wish to use the visualization of the dream gate to help craft a specific dream landscape, look through the dream gate as you make your statement. See the person on the other side of the dream gate, then conjure up a clear and detailed image of the desired dream landscape. Finish by looking through the dream gate to see the target person interacting with the desired landscape. Focus on this image until you can see it with perfect clarity. Then step through the dream gate and interact with both your target person and your target landscape.

Remember that repetition is the key to cuing your unconscious mind so that all these intents and images transfer into your dreams once you fall asleep. Repeat your intentions over and over. As strange as it may seem, shaping the dreamspace can sometimes be as simple making a clear declaration of what you desire to achieve. If you have trouble trusting that your unconscious can pick up on such a simple activity, consider phrasing your declaration like a prayer. Address this to a god of dreams or to whatever deity you feel watches after you (the Dream King, although based on a fictional character, works just fine for me). If you aren't the sort of person who goes for gods and higher powers, address it as a prayer to your Higher Self. If you want to get technical, you are essentially praying to your unconscious anyway in the hopes that it will grant your request.

ACHIEVING LUCIDITY

Through repetition of your target and your intent, you lay the foundations for the dreamwalk in your unconscious mind. All this repetition might seem tedious, but it is necessary for when you seek to dreamwalk from full REM sleep. Classic dreamwalking is the hardest type of dreamwalking to learn how to consciously control, but it also tends to produce the most profound and vivid effects. If you have the patience, repeated practice will pay off. Repeated practice with this method of dreamwalking has another benefit: it can lead to lucid dreaming.

Lucid dreams are those dreams in which you realize that you're dreaming. Learning to lucid dream is the one method of achieving conscious control of the dreamspace while you sleep. This allows you to become an active participant in the dreamspace. Essentially, through lucid dreaming, you become conscious during full REM sleep, controlling the elements of the dream. Once you can combine classic dreamwalking with lucid dreaming, there is almost no limit to what you can achieve in the dreamspace.

There are a number of techniques for achieving lucidity in your dreams, and we will address these in chapter eight. Stephen LaBerge, the modern authority on lucid dreams, has even developed a machine to assist in the process. However, once you fall completely asleep, there is never any guarantee that you will achieve lucid dreams. Your unconscious mind is a tricky place, and navigating that landscape is difficult even for experienced explorers. This is where the second main technique for dreamwalking comes into play: harnessing the hypnagogic state.

CHAPTER SIX

RIDING THE TWILIGHT

I HAVE REFERRED TO SOMETHING CALLED THE "hypnagogic state" several times now. It's a big, imposing word that defines that hazy mental twilight between waking and sleep. Probably everyone who is reading this book has consciously experienced the hypnagogic state at least once. As you begin to fall asleep, you may see patterns of light forming before your eyes. They can create quite a light show on the insides of your eyelids. Starbursts, spirals, diamonds, and a whole host of geometric shapes all manifest as visual hallucinations in the early parts of the hypnagogic state. Though I have no basis of comparison, quite a number of medical writers describe these visual light shows as being similar if not identical to some of the visual hallucinations experienced with the aid of LSD.

The whirling shapes of apparent light, which many have observed before falling asleep, eventually give rise to more complex patterns. As you relax and fall deeper into sleep, these visual images will take the form of faces or butterflies or amazing stellar landscapes. At this point, auditory hallucinations may occur as well, and a number of composers, including Richard Wagner and Giuseppe Tartini, based music on ethereal symphonies heard in the hypnagogic state. Finally, as you drift off into actual sleep, all these amazing experiences give rise to bona fide dreams.

On the other side of the hypnagogic state is the hypnopompic state. "Hypnopompic" roughly translates to "leading out of sleep," and this is the threshold state we experience as we wake up. For some people, the hypnopompic state is a little more lucid that the hypnagogic state, although it is no less of an altered state of consciousness. Also, since you are rested already, it can be easier to do dream work from the hypnopompic state, as you are far less likely to fall fully asleep. Some scientists see no reason to distinguish between the hypnagogic and hypnopompic states, aside from their placement during the sleep cycle. Others suggest that the hallucinatory states experienced in these altered states of consciousness are slightly different. Although, for the sake of simplicity, I will be using "hypnagogic" throughout the rest of the book to refer to the threshold between waking and sleep, understand that you can harness the hypnopompic state in precisely the same way. These two states frame our experience of sleep, and some readers may have more success working from one, while some readers will prefer the other.

WHOLE DREAMING

A few modern scientists believe that these patterns of light and sound are partly what give rise to dreams. In all likelihood, these visual, auditory, and sometimes physical hallucinations arise from tired neurons firing randomly as you relax and make the transition into sleep. It's argued that the only reason this random barrage of sensation begins to take more complex shapes is because our minds, as they relax more deeply into sleep, impose their own patterns upon the experience.

This is based on a psychological concept called the Gestalt principle. *Gestalt* is German for "whole," and in the simplest terms, the Gestalt principle is based on the idea that psychologically we prefer things to be whole and recognizable. When you stare at clouds on a lazy summer day, pointing out to your friend that one looks like a battleship while another looks like the face of your least favorite teacher, you are exercising the Gestalt principle. Although you understand intellectually that the patterns of the clouds are purely random, your mind prefers recognizable things to randomness, and so projects familiar images on the clouds. This is a conscious exercise of the Gestalt principle, but more often than not the effect is subconscious, with the images that you "see" ultimately arising from that hidden portion of your mind.

If we approach the hypnagogic state with the Gestalt principle in mind, we see that your waking mind perceives random patterns, but the more you relax and drift into sleep, the more your subconscious mind takes over, imposing its own order on things. If you haven't started dreaming yet, your conscious mind bears witness to these marvels, watching shapes turn into faces or houses or letters crawling across a page.

Not all of the authorities on dreaming, sleep, and consciousness agree on the nature of hypnagogic hallucinations. The important thing for our studies is that these images are defined as *hallucinations*, and not dreams. When you view something that is not really there, and you're awake, by the standard definition of the term, you're hallucinating. When you view something that's not really there, and you're asleep, you're dreaming. The distinction is more between which mind is in charge and doing the perceiving. The reason that things get so hazy in the hypnagogic state is because not only is it a twilight realm between waking and sleep, but it also seems to be one of the few points where your conscious and subconscious minds freely overlap.

DREAMS AND HALLUCINATIONS

The second, most effective method of intentionally dreamwalking involves harnessing the hypnagogic state so you can dream but still remain conscious of this fact. This is somewhat different from lucid dreaming, where you dream but eventually become aware of the fact that you're dreaming. When you harness the hypnagogic state, you

never completely fall asleep, and therefore you never completely relin-
quish your conscious awareness of what's going on. Instead, you hang
in twilight, partly awake, partly asleep, partly conscious, and partly
given over to your subconscious mind. This is a tricky state to achieve
and it's even harder to maintain, but if you can successfully walk this
balancing beam of consciousness, you can accomplish some truly
amazing feats.

Location is very important to harnessing the hypnagogic state. It's
crucial that you feel both comfortable and safe. For people who practice astral travel, safety is an issue because they tend to become so
detached from their bodies that they lose all sense of what's going on
around those bodies. When dreamwalking in the twilight state, however, safety is an issue for exactly the *opposite* reason.

Due to the nature of the hypnagogic state, you will never quite
lose consciousness, nor will you lose your ability to perceive what's
going on around you. In fact, it's likely that your sense of the world
around you—on many different levels—will become intensely heightened as you approach the hypnagogic state. There is a period of
intense focus as you relax enough to enter this twilight state. Suddenly,
you will be able to hear everything going on in the entire house with
a clarity never experienced before. All sources of light will seem to
grow in intensity until even absolute darkness seems to glow with a
mysterious light. Scents and physical sensations will stand out in ways
you have not experienced them before.

Once you have crossed into the hypnagogic state, your awareness
of this sensory input does not decrease, although it tends to change. As
the lines between dream and reality begin to blur, the way you interpret sensory input can shift, sometimes in disturbing ways. Shadows
passing near the foot of the bed can turn into phantoms reaching out
to you from the abyss. The sound of the television from a distant room
can become murmuring voices calling your name over and over again.
While not all of the sensory input ends up being filtered through a
nightmare lens, there is no real way to predict what impressions your
mind will spin from what's going on around you.

It's important to note that night terrors and the phenomenon known as a Hag attack, in which the sleeper feels the sense of a presence in the room, a feeling of a great weight, typically centered on the chest, that presses the sleeper into the bed, a sense of paralysis, and an overwhelming sense of terror or dread are both thought to be tied to the hypnagogic state. Hag attacks are often preceded by a tingling sensation that washes through the entire body. Sometimes this is described as unpleasant, like the prickly feeling one gets in a limb that's fallen asleep. More often than not, however, it's actually described in pleasant and even sensual terms, as a rippling or a vibration that softly encompasses the whole body. Only when the sensation of being pressed into the bed manifests, along with the impression of a presence in the room, does the Hag attack typically begin to frighten the person experiencing it.

David Hufford, author of *The Terror that Comes in the Night*, identifies the tingling sensation that precedes Hag attack as a physical hallucination connected with the hypnagogic state. Curiously, the sensation is markedly close to Robert Monroe's "vibrational state," which he described as signaling the start of an out-of-body experience. That Monroe was probably passing from wakefulness into the hypnagogic state just prior to relaxing enough to go out-of-body is likely. However, quite a number of his more scientifically minded critics cite this fact as evidence that all of his experiences were nothing more than hypnagogic hallucinations and dreams mistaken for reality.

Based on my own experiences of the hypnagogic state, I can attest that it is easy to become confused in this twilight state between waking and sleep. Sensations are distorted, and it can be difficult at first to identify what is real and what is simply part of your mind and body drifting into sleep. Repeated experiences with this state, however, coupled with correlating reports from people who were being dreamwalked to, have convinced me that not everything experienced in the hypnagogic state is merely an illusion. The important thing as far as our current studies are concerned is to note the uncertain nature of hypnagogic sensations and to take as much care as possible to control the circumstances in which we experience this state.

THE BALANCING ACT

You are relaxed, but not too relaxed, dressed comfortably, and in a space that is quiet, safe, and conducive to dreamwalking. Prior to this point, you have answered the three main questions that go along with any dreamwalk: who you are dreamwalking to, why you are dreamwalking, and what landscape you plan to use. Now all you have to do is get started.

Although most people will most certainly work from their beds, you may want to consider sitting in a chair for this method of dreamwalking. A straight-backed chair that has enough padding to be comfortable is ideal. Sit with your back straight, head erect and facing forward, feet flat on the ground, and your hands held palms-down on the tops of your legs. This is called the Egyptian position, and if you can call to mind the many images of pharaohs sitting oh-so-properly upon their thrones, you'll have an idea of why. I can't say that I prefer this position for this method of dreamwalking, although I have used it with success. Perhaps the greatest benefit of this position comes to those who have trouble staying awake during their journeys through the borderlands of sleep. Sitting upright in the chair has the added benefit of waking you up if your head drops forward in sleep.

Although there is some danger of falling asleep, I prefer to lay down, even when dreamwalking from the hypnagogic state. If you have set your dreaming chamber up in some room other than your bedroom, consider investing in a futon mattress or at least a yoga mat to stretch out on the floor. Comfort is important, although with this technique you don't want to get so comfortable that you simply fall asleep. Your body temperature will drop as you slip into the dream-state, so consider covering yourself with a blanket or at the very least keeping a blanket handy. One of the benefits of using the hypnagogic state to dreamwalk is that you can pull yourself out of things fairly easily, adjust your physical surroundings, and then return almost immediately to the dreamspace.

Laying flat on your back, as opposed to any other position, seems to be most conducive to dreamwalking, regardless of technique. I used to think that this was just a matter of personal preference, but I've found that Don Henrie, another friend who excels at dreamwalking, also prefers starting his journeys by lying on his back in bed, as do several other acquaintances.

Another side note about this position: Melita Denning and Osbourne Phillips, in their book *Astral Projection*, caution against crossing your arms or legs when you are trying to go out-of-body. Although they never fully explain the reasons behind this warning, it is repeated several times in big, bold letters throughout the text. I am going to support their suggestion that you keep your arms and legs free and uncrossed during this exercise, although I don't think it requires any kind of dire warning. The plain and simple fact is that you'll have more success opening yourself to outside connections and sending a portion of yourself out if you keep your body similarly open. Crossing your arms and legs holds your energy in, and I actually recommend it when performing the centering exercise of "Closing the Circuit." If you stretch out in a loose spread-eagle on the bed, you keep your energy open and flowing, providing yourself with the best circumstances to be receptive to this experience.

Once you have settled into a comfortable position, do some rhythmic breathing to help get yourself into a deeply relaxed and focused state. Continue to concentrate on the rhythm of your breathing, allowing this to lull you into a progressively more relaxed state. When your limbs begin to grow heavy, do not fight the sensation. When it feels as if your body is so heavy that it's sinking into the bed, relax into this sensation. As you do, call to mind your dream haven. Imagine yourself standing there, in front of your dream gate. Maintain your sense of connection to the target person and use this to call up their image in the dream gate. Allow your focus on this person be your anchor to consciousness. Feel the dreamspace pressing close as your body continues to slip deeper into the hypnagogic state, but do not let your focus on your target and your intent to contact that person slip away.

As you continue to breathe slowly and evenly, lights and colors may begin to dance before your eyes, and your body will begin to tingle. If you let the sensation just happen without fighting or reacting to it, this will be pleasant and serve to relax you even further. Your body will grow so heavy and so relaxed that it will seem almost impossible to move it. It probably won't even occur to you to try. Dancing lights and flashes of images behind your eyes will herald your arrival to the hypnagogic state. These will seem to be layered on top of the image of your dream haven and you may even seem to physically see the details of that space flickering on the insides of your eyelids.

The biggest problem facing you at this point will be maintaining your mental balance while in this state, hanging intentionally halfway between waking and sleep. This can be tricky, and it will likely take practice to really get the hang of. When you feel as if your body has fallen asleep around you and your mind is caught halfway between wakefulness and dreams, renew your focus on the target person, trying to see his or her image through the dream gate.

The space on the other side of the gate is misty and indistinct. As you slip deeper and deeper into the hypnagogic state, images begin to ripple on the air in the space within the gate. Focus on your connection to the target person. In your mind, call this person's name so it echoes across the gate. At you speak the name, the gate ripples and the mists converge upon a scene. All elements in the image are indistinct save one: you can see your target clearly. The further you slip into the hypnagogic state, the clearer this image becomes. As you relax and allow the dreamscape to form around you, you can see your target with almost perfect clarity, standing on the other side of the gate. The person seems more real by the minute, until the final ripple passes from the air within the gate. You stretch out your hand and the hand of your target clasps your fingers. You are drawn through the dream gate to stand face-to-face with your target. There is no travel involved, just a sort of sideways mental step.

ALTERNATE PATHWAYS

If the Gate of Dreams visualization doesn't seem to work for you, there are several visualizations you can engage in to help close the mental distance between you and your target. You can try any of these from the hypnagogic state (they can also be used as presleep visualizations for classic dreamwalking).

THE TIES THAT BIND:

Focus on the link you have with the target person. With your eyes closed and without releasing the borderline state, find where this link attaches to your own subtle body. Test the energy of the link to insure that this is the person you want. If you aren't sure, extend your perception down the link far enough to sense who is on the other end. Once you have verified that this is your target's link, firmly take the link in both hands and start pulling it to you. Imagine that you are pulling the link hand over hand, as if it were a rope tethering the other person to you. You can accompany this with the appropriate physical motions, although I caution against it, as this can easily interrupt the delicate borderline state. When you have reached the end of the link, you will have closed the conceptual distance between you and your target. Using this link, pull your target through the gate and into your dream haven. If you have crafted a different dreamspace, pull them into that instead. Continue to ride the hypnagogic state, treating the person as if they were right beside you.

SPIDER IN A WEB:

Another method that harnesses the link you have with the target involves thinking of that link as a strand of spiderweb. Imagine that you are a spider, and all the links you have with all the people you have built connections with stretch out around you like a finely glowing web. Like a spider, you can feel the subtle vibrations of each of these strands, and with little effort, you can identify who is on the other end. Focus on the strand that connects you to your target, and imagine a part of yourself moving along the web, closing the conceptual distance between you and your target.

CYBER VISIONS:

There is a variation on the spider technique that might appeal to those with a more technological bent. Links function just like wires. They are tiny, subtle filaments that transfer energy back and forth. Much of this energy is encoded information: how the person on the other end of the link feels, what the person's health is like, what the person is thinking. Given that thought is energy and the aspect of yourself that you plan on sending into dreams is energy, you can send this encoded information through the link as easily as anything else. Focus on your energy and your intent, then ride the wire down to your target.

CALLING THE NAME:

This is another visualization that can be facilitated by a pre-established link but does not require one. This technique relies on a kind of self-hypnosis. As you enter the hypnagogic state, focus on your target. Imagine the person clearly in your mind, and begin to say that person's name, over and over. You may begin by whispering it to yourself, but as you find yourself slipping deeper into the hypnagogic state, actually forming the word with your mouth may become an issue. Once it becomes too hard to concentrate on saying the name out loud—or if you find that actually speaking the name distracts your attention from the hypnagogic state—form the name instead in your mind. Continue the repetitions, holding onto the image of the person in your mind. As more coherent dream images begin to manifest in the hypnagogic state, shape your target's image in your mind. Use your focus on the person's name to make that image real, to draw the person to you.

BREAKING THE ILLUSION:

There is a philosophical principle that distance is an illusion. Either all things are infinitely far apart, or all points are one point. The latter, in some metaphysical instances, seems to be true. This technique of visualization does not involve following links. It simply involves making the space between you and your target not exist. This can be a hard concept to wrap your brain around, but once you manage it, the technique has almost infinite applications. Simply call the target person to mind. Picture the person in your mind's eye with as much clarity of detail as possible. Think about how it feels to be around this person, think about how touching this person would make you feel. Then— and here's the tricky part—*be there*. Forget that there is any distance between you and this other person. Simply reach out and be where that person is.

FURTHER JOURNEYS

Once you have successfully made the connection to your target, through whatever means, most of the hard work is done. What follows after this point will vary from experience to experience and from individual to individual. For the most part, you will retain control over the dream images, and in this respect, it will feel as if you are still just repeating the visualization you prepared before starting out. However, there will be elements that manifest all on their own, and sometimes these will surprise you with their novelty and vividness.

The key for success is balance. Focus too hard, and you will tip the balance to consciousness. This will pull you out of the dream so all you are doing is running through a visualization in your head. If you let yourself relax too completely into the dream, however, you are likely to slip into sleep, and then you lose the conscious control of the experience. You want to maintain a twilight state throughout the whole experience. Not only should you feel both asleep and awake, but you should also be able to feel as if you are both dreaming and directing the dream—an observer and a participant all at once.

The first several times you attempt this sort of "travel," keep the journey simple and short. Make contact with your target and instigate some interaction that the person will be likely to remember once they wake up. When you return back through the Gates of Dream and the hypnagogic state, rouse yourself, allowing your body to come slowly out of sleep. Don't be surprised if the heavy, unresponsive feeling in your limbs lingers for a while. Fine motor control may take a little while to return, and you are likely to remain hypersensitive to just about any kind of sensory input. Taking a few moments to go through a grounding exercise will help return you to yourself. Once you feel a bit more balanced and "here," write down your experience, taking care to record any unusual details. Record the time, the date, and the person that you walked to. By comparing your experiences against those of the people you walk to, you will learn how to judge the overall success of your dreamwalking activities.

WHITE ELEPHANTS

If you are in a mood to experiment, get a willing partner to participate in a series of dreamwalks. When you set up the dream landscape of the meeting space, add one or two elements that are striking and unusual—a big white elephant, for example.

Write down a description of the dream landscape you intend to construct, including the detail of the white elephant. Note the time, the date, and the name of your target. As you do your presleep visualization, come back to the image of the white elephant again and again, until it has become firmly planted in the overall landscape of the dream.

Don't tell your target what it is they're looking for in the dream. Just wait to see what details they remember from the dreamwalk. Repeat the process over several nights, using the same imagery, and see when—or if—your target notices the elephant.

CHAPTER SEVEN

REMEMBERING YOUR DREAMS

IT'S A PSYCHOLOGICAL FACT THAT THE MORE you focus on your dreams, the more likely you are to remember them. Also, the more attention you pay to them, the more vivid your dreams will become. This became very evident to me as I was writing this book. Sleeping became just an extension of my daytime work (although it was convenient to be able to justify sleeping in late as "research"). Since I was focused on the subject of dreams, my subconscious happily obliged me by filling each sleep cycle with experiences that were vivid, symbolic, and increasingly strange.

Over the course of the month of November, I spent time with a shirtless Patrick Stewart at a camping resort, fought zombies in my old high school, helped my aunt repair the engine in an old truck that was having trouble going up a steep hill, helped instruct friends in the proper way to act as characters in a haunted asylum, and took flight through my old neighborhood, zipping past houses and trees. While my dream life is usually quite vivid, particularly around this time of year, this was exceptional even for me. I was averaging three or four lengthy dreams each night, all of them with vivid characters and fully developed plotlines. On the bright side, there was little temptation to sit and watch TV. I had all the entertainment I needed in sleep.

Not everyone has such luck at remembering their dreams. Many people will assert that they don't even dream. This is a misconception, as REM sleep, the stage in which we dream, is a fundamental part of natural sleep. If we don't get a certain amount of REM in each night, we won't feel rested in the morning. Studies have shown that if people are deprived of REM sleep for long periods of time, it leads to waking hallucinations and mental instability.

If everyone dreams, then why is it that some people can recall such vivid adventures while others feel as if their minds simply turn off in sleep? In some cases, it comes down to attitude. Creative people, for the most part, have rich dream lives, and many of them draw additional inspiration from their dreams. Robert Louis Stevenson's *Dr. Jekyll and Mr. Hyde* was written almost completely in a dream, and Mary Shelley's *Frankenstein* owes much of its inspiration to a dream. Because writers and poets and artists base their careers upon the stuff of imagination, they tend to have a positive approach to the fanciful material encountered in dreams. Dreams are not only remembered, but they are also mined for inspiration and meaning.

People with a more rational approach to reality are less likely to remember their dreams, mainly because they do not attribute any worth to these surreal images that play through the mind each night. The memory of a dream is a fragile thing, often shattered entirely with the blaring of an alarm clock or washed down the drain as we shower in the morning. If you don't pay attention to the fragile images that linger in your mind upon waking, they will retreat back into the subconscious realm from which they came, only to manifest again once the conscious mind is lost to sleep.

Since attitude plays such a significant role in our memory of dreams, it's important first to decide that your dreams are worth remembering. Feeling as if dreams are nothing more than nonsense images that occupy you while you sleep will hardly be helpful to this endeavor. Once you have decided that your dreams may be worth remembering, the next thing you need to do is to simply start paying attention. There are a couple of steps you can use to start remembering your dreams with greater clarity.

MEDITATE ON YOUR DREAMS:

Each morning when you wake up, don't just jump right out of bed. When you have the luxury of time, allow yourself to hang in that comfortable, half-awake state. While in this state, you are much more likely to retain lingering traces of your dreams. If you have some image still hanging in your mind from a dream, grab onto it. Give the image all of your focus and ask yourself what it's connected to and what it might mean. As you turn the dream shard around in your mind, you may find that other fragments connected to this first one quite naturally return to your consciousness. Follow the trail of dream shards as far as they go, piecing together as much of the dream as you can.

DIAL IN YOUR DREAMS:

The more you focus on your dreams, the more you will remember them and the more vivid they will become. You can take advantage of this by focusing on your dreams before you fall asleep at night. Decide that you are going to dream. Call to mind dreams you remember from the past, even if these are long-distant, childhood dreams. Put yourself clearly into the mindset of dreaming. Remember what it felt like, being in a dream. Try to recapture that feeling as you drift off to sleep. As you focus on dreaming before falling asleep, you can even suggest content for your dreams. Think about what you'd like to encounter in your dreams, then hold this thought close as you surrender to sleep.

TALK ABOUT YOUR DREAMS:

According to anthropologist Kilton Stewart, the Senoi tribe of Malaysia had a very special relationship with their dreams. The whole tribe had a tradition of openly discussing their dreams. At the start of every day, they would sit around and discuss the events they had experienced while they slept, accepting that these events had intrinsic meaning. If a Senoi had dreamed of another member of the tribe, he or she was encouraged to go meet and speak with this person and resolve any conflicts suggested by the dream. Stewart asserted that the tribe's attitude toward dreams and dreaming kept this small ethnic group psychologically healthy and almost completely crime free. The actual reality of the Senoi tribe and their dreaming habits has been a matter of much dispute in both the psychological and anthropological communities. Real or not, the Senoi do have an example to set for us. Talking to friends and sharing your dreams is another way to expand your awareness of your nightly journeys. Find someone you trust and share your dreams. Encourage this person to do the same. If you dream about someone you know, consider sharing the dream with that person. You never know when you'll discover that you both dreamed the same thing.

Dreams may not seem rational, but they do have meaning, and they should be approached as legitimate experiences. Once you have worked up enough curiosity to take a serious look at your dreams, the next most useful method for developing dream recall is to start a journal of your dreams.

DREAM JOURNALING

The idea of keeping a journal always intimidates some people. They can come up with a billion and one reasons why they can't keep a journal, from the fact that they don't have the time to the fact that writing just isn't their thing. And yet a dream journal remains one of the best methods for not only remembering your dreams but also growing to understand them. If you really want to master the art of dreamwalking, you're going to have to keep a dream journal, if for no other reason than to keep track of your dreamwalking experiences.

Your dream journal does not have to be a great work of literature. No one but you ever has to see this journal, and so you really shouldn't worry about your grammar or spelling or how badly you feel you describe things. The important thing about a dream journal is that you make an effort to record your dreams.

If there was some overriding requirement that a dream journal be legible, I'd certainly be in trouble. I keep my dream journal by my bed, and it's not uncommon for me to wake up from a dream, grab a pen and just start scribbling down details without ever turning on a light in my room. While I have developed some skill for writing in the dark, the journal entries that are made this way are always pretty difficult to read. Somehow, I always manage to write them diagonally across the page, leaving huge gaps of space between lines because I'm afraid of writing on top of things.

While spelling and neatness are not crucial to your journal, you do want to be careful about times and dates. This is doubly important if it's your intention to use your dream journal to verify dreamwalking experiences. While it can be very compelling to learn that a friend dreamed about you on the same night you dreamed about them, it becomes even more convincing if you can refer back to your journal and note the exact time, along with details that correlate to your friend's dream.

How thorough you want to get in your descriptions of dreams will be up to you. For the most part, you want to attempt to capture the main images of the dream, plus any overriding feelings or sensations you associated with it. If you attempt to interpret some of the meaning of the dream, be sure to distinguish this section from the actual record of the dream. An ideal dream entry will not attempt to impose any meaning on the dream. Instead, it will simply record the dream as you remember it with as much detail as possible. You can analyze it all you want once the details are written down.

Keep in mind that dreams do not always make logical sense, nor do they always follow a linear progression of events. This can make it very hard to write out a record of the dream, as you'll find yourself trying to explain in the journal how you went from talking to a spider to dancing on top of the Eiffel Tower. In the dream, there was probably no transition at all between these two events, and yet the transition made sense at the time. It's okay in your journal to say, "I have no idea how I got there, but then I was on top of the Eiffel Tower." Also, if you know there was a transition, but you've forgotten it since waking, make a note that there's some forgotten material, and move along to what you do remember. You might find that by the time you've written the clearer details down, some of the fuzzier material has returned to you. You can always go back and expand upon the fuzzy parts later.

If you want to capture as much detail from a dream as possible, write it down as soon as you wake up from it. This means that, if you wake up in the night from a dream, you should grab your journal and write down the details while they're still fresh in your memory. If you just roll over and go back to sleep, you may find it very difficult to remember every aspect of that dream in the morning. You are always most likely to remember the dream you were having just prior to waking up, and if you wait until morning, then it's highly probable that another dream will take its place.

Once you wake up, try not to pull yourself immediately out of that dreamy half-asleep state. Have you ever noticed how a dream can be very vivid in your mind while you're still lying in bed, but once you get done with your morning shower you can't even remember it any more? Part of the reason for this is the change in consciousness you go through as you become fully awake. When you get out of bed, your mind immediately starts focusing on other things, and the content of your dreams will fade back into the subconscious from whence it came. For a vivid and healthy dream life, give yourself enough time in the morning to lay in bed for five or ten minutes, just thinking about your dreams. Close your eyes and try to conjure up the feeling you had in your dreams. Ask yourself, "What was I just dreaming?" and let your mind replay as much as possible from the night before. After this exercise, grab your dream journal and record it all, because as soon as you hit the shower, much of the detail will go away.

One way to force yourself to have vivid dreams is to wake up from a full sleep cycle, and then roll over and go back to sleep. Throughout the night, the amount of time spent in REM increases. The first dreams of the night last approximately ten minutes, while the dreams you have just prior to waking up can last as long as thirty minutes. By going back to sleep, you put yourself into an extended REM cycle, and this almost guarantees a lengthy stretch of vivid dreams.

MINING THE DREAMSPACE

I mentioned in the beginning of this chapter that one of the benefits of writing this book was that sleeping in could be justified as research. To complete this section, I wanted to include a sample of my own dream journal. Normally, I record my dreams right after I wake up, but this means that I usually only remember the last dream or two of the night. I wanted to present a full cycle of dreaming, so I could cover a variety of dreams. To this end, I set a day aside just to devote to dreaming. Each time I woke up from a dream, I would make note of it, then go back to sleep in search of more dreams.

Let me preface this by saying that my dreams are not always this interesting, complex, or vivid. There are some days where my dreams are hardly worth mentioning, and the pallid, jumbled images fade quickly from my mind. But there are times when, for weeks, I will dream vividly and often each time I go to sleep. Sometimes I refer to these times as a "dream storm," especially if I learn that a number of my friends are also experiencing an increase in the frequency and vividness in their dreams.

Dream storms happen when a spate of unusually vivid dreams manifest for a group of dreamers over several nights in a row. As an active dreamer, however, it's possible to intentionally cause such a "storm." For myself, when I want to spice up my dream life, I literally put in a request. In classic dreamwalking, we saw how one can prime the subconscious by focusing on things just prior to falling asleep. You do not have to limit yourself just to focusing on dreamwalking. You can focus on remembering your dreams. You can focus on having pleasant dreams instead of nightmares, and you can focus on becoming lucid in your dreams. You can also essentially put in a request to your subconscious to make your dreams more interesting that night— a request I've made on several occasions that have proven both enlightening and entertaining.

Because it often feels a little strange to make a request of one's own subconscious mind, I usually address my requests to the Dream King.

Anyone who's read Neil Gaiman's storytelling masterpiece, the *Sandman* series, knows that Lord Morpheus of the Endless is essentially the King of the Dreaming. Morpheus, of course, gets his name from the Greek god of dreams, child of Hypnos, god of sleep, and Nox, goddess of night. Although he is merely a character in a graphic novel series, the archetype of the Dream King is so eloquently captured in Gaiman's Morpheus, that he speaks very deeply to me. If I picture Morpheus in my mind just prior to sleep and make a request of the Dream King, all I'm doing is priming my subconscious with that same request, but the potency of the image makes the exercise much more effective for me. I can say, "I want to have interesting dreams tonight," but if I pray to the Dream King for a night full of dreams, I've already set the stage for something colorful and creative.

The following entries, recorded on November 29, 2005, reflect a bumper crop of images sown by the Dream King. I've put this section together to reflect what an ideal dream journal should look like, presenting the records of the dreams themselves first and including interpretation and commentary only after all the details of each dream have been set down. I was pretty excited about this one day's worth of dreaming, because the exercise obliged me with good examples of several different types of dreams. And even though it was not my expressed intention to dreamwalk, the final dream of the cycle might have been something very interesting indeed.

DREAM #1

I'm standing at the dining room table. It's December, and I'm getting ready to go to classes. I'm in college again, and it's near the end of the semester. There's a class that I haven't gone to all semester. I don't even remember the course number or what room it's supposed to meet at. I am worrying about this class, because I'm running out of time to drop it so it won't affect my grade. As I look down at bills and papers on the dining room table, I decide that I'm going to take care of dropping that class when I drive to the college later. I want to write myself a note so I don't forget, but I have trouble finding paper that isn't already covered with writing. I finally grab an old flyer from one of my annual spring workshop events. It's lime green, and I fold it over to write on the back.

The paper must be really thin, though, because all the letters from the front of the sheet bleed through to the back, making it hard to read what I've just written. I'm running out of time, however, so I can't stop to look for a better piece of paper. I trace back over my note to myself several times with the black pen I found. There are two things I write down to remember: "world religions," which is the title of the class I have to drop, and something else that I can't remember. I'm still not happy with how the note is written and I worry that I'll be unable to read it later. But now I'm running late, so I need to go. Somewhere on my way to the car, I find a red sharpie marker, so I trace over my note with this. That stands out so I can read it. As I try to read the second part of the note to myself, I wake up.

COMMENTARY DREAM #1

I've been out of college for a decade now, but I can't count the number of times that I've had some variation of this dream. It's pretty clear that this is an anxiety dream, although typically the subject of the class is math—a subject I never liked and always had trouble with. It was interesting that this time the subject of the missed class in this dream was "world religions." In contrast to math, this has always been a major area of interest for me, and it's a subject in which I excel. Several days before having this dream, however, a dispute arose about how many credit hours I actually had in the religious studies part of my degree. It was a friendly dispute, but at the time it opened old wounds regarding some conflicts I had with professors and administrators at my old college. The issue concerning my religious studies classes obviously manifested in this dream.

It is also interesting that I kept having trouble writing a note to myself in this dream. This is a reflection of more anxiety, this time about the book I'm working on. The day before the dreaming experiment I did not get as much writing done as I would have liked, and I felt like I was endlessly rewriting this one section. The fact that I was finally able to write an acceptable note with a red marker is also significant—I kept telling myself that I should stop worrying about the troublesome section, as the current work was only a rough draft. Everything could be fixed during the editorial process. Notably, the traditional tool of the editor is a red pen.

This dream very neatly demonstrates several important things. First, our unconscious is known to use our dreams to work out issues and conflicts that our waking mind can't solve. This is how Friedrich August Kekule von Stradonitz fell asleep and discovered the structure of the benzene ring, and how Eli Whitney dreamed of the proper design of needles for his famous sewing machine. Dreams are often viewed as the mind's way of cataloging the thoughts and experiences from the previous day, sorting them out through meaningful images.

The fact that dreams speak to us somewhat indirectly through the medium of symbols is also reflected in this dream. This dream was obtained while doing work on a book, and the process of writing was heavily on my mind. Although my main concern was with a specific work, the dream focuses instead on the very process of writing, of putting letters down on a piece of paper. To be honest, this is a fairly direct symbol for a dream. In many cases, it might take a little creativity to discover what a dream image really means. In *Our Dreaming Mind*, Robert Van de Castle cites one dream in which a woman preparing for surgery is afraid of walking on brittle window panes—a fact that he sees as a play on the word "pain," something she was also afraid of prior to surgery.

DREAM #2

I am driving through a park, going down a little asphalt road to a wooden pavilion. There are trees everywhere. It must be fall, because the road and parking lot are full of leaves. I park my car and go into the pavilion, but as I approach, I notice that it's not an open-air pavilion like I thought. It has screens and windows. It's actually a house. I get the sense that I am meeting people here, or that I'm supposed to. I go up to the little house—it's very dark inside. I think I've seen something like it before. It's only a one-story affair, with screens stretched between big supports of dark red wood.

There are no lights on inside the house. The only light is what comes in through the windows and the open door. This isn't much—it's very gray outside, an overcast fall afternoon. There is a little old lady living here. I don't know her name, but I'm here to do something for her. I think I might work for some agency. We check in on the elderly, help them out, keep them company. The lady seems very thin and pale, ghostlike. My attention is drawn to a door leading down to a very steep set of steps. I know this is the basement. The steps seem to disappear into a black pit. No light gets down there. I don't want to look down those steps, but the door to the basement isn't a wood door. It's an old metal screen door with a pitted aluminum frame. It has glass instead of screens. I'm glad there is at least something between me and the basement.

I think I'm in the kitchen now. There's still almost no light in the house. It doesn't occur to me to look for a light switch. My cat Cornelius comes up to me.

Somehow he's here. He's hungry and thirsty. The old lady has a bowl of water on the kitchen counter. It's one of those cat fountains, that cycles and filters the water. The counter is too high up for Cornelius. He's old and I'm worried he can't jump that high without hurting himself. I grab the bowl of water to set it on the floor. It has no plug connecting it to an outlet, and this puzzles me for a moment, because I can see the water being churned by some internal device. There is also something at the bottom of the bowl. I peer in and it looks like whole wheat pasta shells, uncooked. I have no idea what they're doing in there, and I'm not sure if the water's good. I smell it, and it seems fine, so I place it on the floor for Cornelius.

The old lady of the house scolds me because water and food can't go directly on the floor. I think she has mice or something. So I compromise and put it up on a little metal shelf that is just above the floor. Cornelius should be able to reach it without difficulty. There are kitchen gadgets on the shelf, a wire rack, old-style eggbeater, some other things. Cornelius goes and drinks the water.

I think I wake up a little, but then I go back to the dream. Now I'm with an old man. It's a different house, still dark, lots of wood paneling. We're standing in a kitchen. He looks very old and frail. There are liver spots on his bald head. Someone else is there with me, and she asks him how old he is. I think she is another agent working with me. She's older than me, maybe in her forties, plump, hair beginning to go gray. She has a clipboard. He can't remember how old he is right away. He starts counting. He says, "1917," several times, and I get the impression that he was born in that year. But when he's finished calculating, he says he's sixty-eight. He looks so much older.

COMMENTARY DREAM #2

It's not uncommon for me to have story dreams—dreams where I both am and am not myself, and am cast in a role in some unfolding tale. This one is less coherent than most of the story dreams I've had, several of which have provided enough material to become full-blown novels. Story dreams have only the barest of obvious connections to my waking life, and they typically follow a linear progression of events (as opposed to many dreams that just seem to flip back and forth randomly between various images). This one had less of a cohesive story than most, though it was still fairly linear except for the jump in events when I woke up and fell back asleep.

The theme of the dream is old age, and this is the one main theme I c[...] tie back to my waking life. I've had my cat, Cornelius, since the fall o[...] and we've never been certain how old he was when he came to [...]

has been a matter of some debate recently, especially since we've started to notice that he limps a little going up and down the stairs, as if arthritis is beginning to settle into his back hips.

Aside from Cornelius and the issue of age, none of the other elements of the dream really seem connected to my waking reality. I did not recognize any of the people in the dream, and the houses, although greatly detailed, were unfamiliar to me.

Story dreams have long puzzled me, especially as several of mine seem to take place in the same "world," with recurring characters and themes. I find them puzzling for two reasons. First, because they are so much more coherent than typical dreams, it always seems as if they should have some significant meaning. Secondly, there have been occasions where friends seem to remember similar, if not identical, story dreams. Despite this, story dreams do not have the feel of dreamwalking, nor do they have the feel of prophetic dreams. The dreams are more like movies that the mind has conjured up from a variety of sources in order to entertain.

From a psychological perspective, there is probably a simple reason for why many of my story dreams resemble one another and why they also resemble dreams reported by friends. Much of the material of story dreams is archetypal. That is to say, it is built upon widespread themes that each of us has been exposed to. In the views of psychologist Carl Jung, these dreams draw upon the collective unconscious, a vast storehouse of themes and images that all humans share because of the fundamental shared humanness of our experiences. The classic Jungian dream that this particular story dream reflects is the house dream, where the dreamer is exploring a house, often discovering extensive, hidden portions up in the attic or down in the basement. By Jung's understanding, the house is merely a symbol of the self, and the exploration signifies the sleeper's journey of exploring him or herself. The dark, hidden spaces correlate neatly to portions of the psyche that have been hidden or locked away, particularly the unconscious mind itself.

Ap— think the other lady working with me represents my Aunt Rita. of social work I remember her doing, and some of my first nces were helping her deal with the elderly.

DREAM #3

Something about cars, my new white car. I left my car parked outside some-where. I need it to go home. I have the keys, but when I go out, the car isn't where I left it. This sounds strange, but as I'm looking for it, I'm asking for "Old Wormwood." I call my great-aunt on my cell phone. I don't expect her to answer the phone because she's still driving. Somehow, I can see her in her car, driving, although I'm not there. But then she answers the phone in her car. This is strange, because I didn't think she had a cell phone. But I don't worry about it. I yell at her for leaving me the keys but no car, and I ask her to come pick me up. Then I'm in the car with her and we're driving. I'm not clear what she did with my car. We're riding in hers, which is much smaller.

COMMENTARY DREAM #3

This jumbled and almost nonsensical dream stands in direct contrast to the straightforward and linear action of the story dream that preceded it. Writing the dream out gave it much more cohesion than it actually possessed. It was more a series of images, only partially connected by logical actions. The detail of the car's name, "Old Wormwood," is especially puzzling, although it can be traced to my waking life. About two weeks before the dream, an old friend came to visit. He brought with him an old bottle of absinthe, which I had taught him to make with anisette liqueur and wormwood, an herb. The bottle was left outside my room, untouched.

This is a good example of a typical surreal dream. Parts of it make some sense, but they are often juxtaposed with nonsense. The action also does not follow a linear progression, but jumps around. Often, there are also changes in perspective, like talking on the phone one minute, then seeing my great-aunt driving from a third-person perspective the next.

Dreams like this can be frustrating. They leave the dreamer with an impression that there is some deeper meaning, but that meaning is impossi-ble to fathom. Personally, I get dreams like this most often when I am pro-cessing new habits or new information. The white car is fairly new to me, and I'm still getting adjusted to the thought that it's mine. Cell phones remain these mysterious gadgets that I need to make use of but am too technologi-cally challenged to really master. The fact that I called someone on a cell phone in a dream tells me that some part of my brain is trying to integrate the notion that cell phones are for communicating. Notably, one of the other main purposes that psychologists attribute to dreams is the function of mov-ing material from short-term memory to long-term memory.

DREAM #4

I wake up and consider getting out of bed. I think about all the dreams I've already had, and I'm curious what else I might dream about. I roll over and try to fall back asleep. As I drift off, I see a little penguin waddling across a backdrop of black nothingness. The penguin is white and gray, like a puffy penguin chick. It's very comical, and I realize that it's an actor in a suit, or maybe a clown. It has plumes on either side of its eyes, yellow and orange. I think I recognize it from a movie trailer.

COMMENTARY DREAM #4

The significance of this dream was the fact that I actually started having it while I was still awake. The little penguin started as an image of whirling lights on the insides of my eyelids—a hypnagogic hallucination. It was by focusing on this whirling circle of gray and white that I forced myself back into dreams. As I slid from the edge of waking consciousness to sleep, the whirling dot grew gradually more complicated in its shape and behavior, until it was a little marching penguin. There's no background to the image because the penguin never developed completely into a dream—it was just an image I saw in the darkness, against the insides of my eyelids.

Although I don't normally hallucinate in penguin-vision, it really came as no surprise, given the timing. I had recently seen a trailer for some computer animated penguin movie and this was followed almost immediately by a Coca-Cola ad that involved another computer animation with penguins.

This little snippet is a good example of a hypnagogic "dream." They typically focus on one fairly simple image, beginning with geometric shapes. There is little to no background detail (the image often seems as if it's floating in space), and no real "story" to speak of. The dreamer might impose some kind of meaning on the image, which manifests not as a series of actions but simply as background information that is known in the dream. In the case of the penguin, this is demonstrated by the sudden realization that the penguin is in fact an actor or clown in a penguin suit, although nothing in the image itself really indicates this.

DREAM #5

I'm at one of my workshops. People are talking and milling about in the background. I'm at a table or desk, sorting through paperwork. I'm looking at a check. It hasn't been made out properly, and I'm wondering if I can cash it. It's from someone named "Angel," and it's for the workshop. I think Angel put a bunch of numbers in the wrong place, like a serial number or something. Then I look and see that the amount reads, "23.46," which is apparently the exact cost of attending the workshop. I thought it was a serial number because it looked longer because of the writing, and I didn't see the decimal point right away. I want to get this person to correct the check, but I've been told they haven't showed up at the workshop.

A willowy blond girl comes up to me, interrupting my contemplation of the check. There were other things going on in this dream, but they all seem to fade away when she walks up to me. I am aware of her and me now, no one else. I am no longer holding the check.

The girl looks about twenty and has long, straight blond hair and very pale skin. She's very thin, in an attractive but coltish way. She's wearing a very short taupe skirt and a beige tank top. No jewelry, no makeup. I know she's someone new who has not attended this workshop. She pulls on my sleeve and tells me that she came to see me and that she brought someone I know. This person told her how to find me. I have to go see him now, because she' going to have to leave with him soon. She won't tell me where he is; she needs to take me to him.

She takes me downstairs. There's a sense of movement, and now we're in the family room of the house I grew up in. The huge old television set is in its usual place up against the wall, looking dusty, as always. I see a young man sitting in front of the television, playing a modern video game. His hair is also blond, longish with a little wave, not quite down to his shoulders. I can tell he had short hair not too long ago, and he started to grow it back out. I don't recognize him from behind. Then he says, "Hey stranger. It's been a while." He turns away from the television screen, and I recognize his face. He's someone I haven't seen in several years.

I'm glad he came, and I rush over to give him a big hug. The room spins as I hug him, and I close my eyes, but it keeps spinning. I get his hair in my face. It's coarser than I expected. His hair is why I didn't recognize him. He's wearing it differently from what I remember, and I think it's been dyed. At least, there's something brassy, almost reddish to the blond in places. He's lost weight as well, but not in a bad way. I can feel ribs and muscle under his shirt as I'm hugging him. "I can't stay long," he tells me. "But I've missed you," I respond.

This feels real, like a dreamwalk. I don't want him to go away again.

I put my face close to his. He hasn't shaved in a while, and his jaw and throat are all stubbly. I'm not sure if this looks good on him. I keep looking into his eyes. I'm afraid if he goes with the willowy girl, I won't see him again for a very long time. She's waiting at the door. I can see a light behind her, coming *in through the doorway. It makes her look like something from another world. She looks impatient, shifting from foot to foot, but her face is still very pleasant, very serene. When I focus on him, I almost forget she's there, she's so quiet. But she won't go away. She just waits. Finally, she taps him on the shoulder and says gently, "We have to leave." Even as the words are spoken, I wake up. There's no sense of being jolted awake, but there's no sense of the dream ending. It just stops and I'm awake, holding my pillow and blankets the way I remember holding him in the dream. I try to fall back into the dream to talk to him some more, but though I can get back to the family room, he's nowhere to be seen.*

COMMENTARY DREAM #5

This dream was fairly intense and personal. Although I did not set out to dreamwalk this night, it seems something very interesting happened. I strongly suspect that this was an instance of dreamwalking, and a fairly unusual one at that.

First, with dream #4 that immediately preceded this, I intentionally reentered the dreamspace after fully waking up. I entered this dream from the hypnagogic state, willing myself to move from waking to sleep. Once I let go of full, waking consciousness, I started off in a fairly ordinary dream. I'm at an event and I'm fretting about money. As anxieties of various sorts have manifested in nearly all of the previous night's dreams, this is in keeping with the overall pattern of my dreams. I have a check that I might not be able to cash, and while I'm studying this, I am dimly aware of other people in the background. And then an unusual person enters the dream, eclipsing everything else.

Where most of the other people who had appeared in this dream were dim and distant figures, not recognizable as individuals, this girl appears in exceptional detail. I even notice her clothes, which is fairly unusual for me. She has a message for me, and she needs to take me somewhere. As we travel together, the setting of the first dream is replaced with a new setting: the familiar family room from my childhood. This is always a cue for me and typically indicates the default backdrop of my dreamspace. Note, however, that I did not start out here, but was *led* here by another person. This mysterious girl serves as the mediator between me and an old friend. She brought him, but he had to show her how to find me, and she, in turn, must show me how to find him.

Almost as soon as I am in the family room from my childhood, this becomes a lucid dream. I am aware that I am sleeping, and I am aware that I'm interacting with this person in my dreams. In the dream, I note that it feels like a dreamwalk, because his presence is so immediate and real. One of the hallmarks of dreamwalking, at least for me, is that it feels as if I am actually, physically present with the person I am interacting with. If I was not aware on some level that it was a dream, I might mistake it for a perfectly ordinary waking encounter.

In the majority of my dreamwalking experiences, I and the person I've dreamwalked to are the only real presences in the dream. If there is more than one person, I am interacting directly with everyone involved. It's highly unusual for someone to remain in the background and not simply fade away, and yet this mystery girl was a presence in the room with both of us. She stood aside and waited patiently for us to finish interacting, but she never left. Her action brought the dream to an abrupt close. It's not as if I jolted suddenly awake. It felt more like I became aware of lying in my bed because there was suddenly no more dream.

ADDENDUM: Certainly, this incident has all the hallmarks I have come to associate with dreamwalking, from the setting, to the focus on an individual, to the lucidity. However, I don't believe I was the one who initiated this dreamwalk, even though it occurred in my traditional dreaming space. I was led there by this strange girl, who, in the end, seemed to also lead my friend away and end the dream.

This is going to seem strange, but while in the dream, I recognized my friend, once I woke up, I had trouble placing him. I knew that he was known to me, but I know a whole lot of people and sometimes it's hard keeping track of them all. I kept trying to tell myself he was one friend, Phil, because of his build, but the hair and eye color didn't match. This confused me, and I wondered if these things had simply been different in the dream.

And then, with a chill, I realized who I had been holding close to me. The key was in the first part of the dream, the uncashed check that was an unfulfilled promise to attend a gathering.

A young man I knew as Angel died this past September very suddenly of a brain aneurism. We had only seen one another a few brief times, but like most people I feel a connection to, we bonded almost immediately. There was much left undone and unsaid between us. Although he kept promising to visit and make contact with the rest of House Kheperu, life always intervened. He had long, blond hair when I first met him, but he cut it when he went into the military. It came as no surprise to those who knew him that he did not last in the military, and he had been out for quite a while before he died. His hair, still short, had started to grow back in.

In asking around about how Angel looked *when he died*, it seems that he matches the young man in my dream. This is significant to me, because my own image of Angel still retains the long hair and heavier build he had when I met him. We've already covered the fact that the realm of dreams and the realm of spirits overlap. But it seems here that Angel and I had a little help in crossing that boundary. The willowy girl, so remarkable and vivid to me, serves as a psychopomp in this dream. A psychopomp is a spirit guide, someone who leads spirits from the realm of the living to the realm of the dead — and sometimes back again. It's very interesting that she seems to have led Angel into the dreamspace, and then goes and fetches me. She acts as a go-between, and when the time's up, she takes Angel out of the overlapping part of dreamspace, leading him back to wherever he had traveled from.

I've dreamwalked to many people. I've had people dreamwalk to me. I have never had a third party enter my dreams and lead me to someone, especially someone who had died. The Dream King more than met my request for an interesting night of dreams, because this was a wholly new experience, even for me.

DREAM JOURNAL: CONCLUSION

It's important to keep in mind that the above selections are meant as a sample only. Use them as a guideline for keeping your own dream journal, but don't feel as if your work must be identical in format or content. Your own dream journal, especially when you are first beginning to record your dreams, is not likely to be quite so action-packed. It's unusual to dream this vividly each and every night. Realistically, most people will have two or three vivid, fully detailed dreams to record each week.

When describing a dream in your journal, try to recapture that dream as accurately as possible—not only in detail but also in feel. If you go back over the samples I've included, you will see that I've tried to retain the feel of the dream in the language I used to record it. If all you remember about a dream are a few disjointed images, don't try to force those images into a coherent sentence. Simply record the images and sensations as they appear to you in your memory. Dreams don't always make linear sense, and neither will many of the entries in your dream journal.

After recording the essential details of each dream, I wrote down some comments addressing what I thought that dream was about. Note that this commentary is clearly separated from the actual details of the dream. This is one thing you should try to stick to in your own journal. Resist the urge to impose meaning upon a dream while you are recording the raw details that you recall from that dream. Stick to just what you remember. Once you have put that down, then you can mark off a separate part of the entry where you think out loud about what the dream meant.

Do not feel pressured to be absolutely accurate with your dream interpretation. Write down whatever ideas come to mind and understand that you can add more commentary later as more insight or information becomes available. I did this with dream #2, adding an addendum where I suggest that the middle-aged agent helping me with the elderly was a symbol of my Aunt Rita. I might not have thought of this if it weren't for the later dream where she figured so strongly.

You are successfully keeping a good dream journal if:
- You make an effort to record whatever you remember
- You recapture your dreams in feeling as well as detail
- You make honest efforts to understand the dream in your commentary
- You are willing to revise your interpretation when faced with new data

CHAPTER EIGHT

LUCID DREAMS

FROM THE MONKS OF BUDDHIST TIBET to the 12th century Spanish Sufi Ibn El-Arabi, mystics the world over have proclaimed the benefits of lucid dreaming. For religious thinkers, lucid dreaming has long been seen as a way to illuminate both the nature of the Self and the nature of reality. Tibetan Buddhists were pursuing lucid dreams as early as the eighth century C.E. According to their philosophy, the mastery of lucid dreams was a necessary step in the pursuit of enlightenment. The ability to recognize the illusory nature of the dreamstate directly correlated to the ability to recognize the illusory nature of all things. The same methods used to gain control over dreams could be applied to controlling the illusion of waking reality.

In keeping with this mystical aspect of lucid dreams, it's been proven that people who practice meditation also have a high likelihood of achieving lucidity in their dreams. Additionally, dream researcher Jayne Gackenbach has demonstrated a correlation between people who have had NDEs and people who lucid dream. Does this suggest, as the Tibetans believe, that the dreamspace is related to the Between, so that the process of moving from waking consciousness to dreams is paralleled by the process of moving from the world of the living to the world of the dead?

WIDE-AWAKE SLEEPING

The first written description of a lucid dream can be attributed to Saint Augustine who, in 415 C.E, recorded the experience for the Roman physician Gennadius. In 1867, French researcher Hervey Saint-Denys coined the term *rêve lucide* (lucid dream). Although Saint-Denys was technically the first major thinker in the modern era to seriously study the phenomenon of lucid dreams, Dutch psychiatrist Frederick Van Eeden is still more frequently associated with the development of the term. Van Eeden was doing research on dreaming between the years of 1898 and 1912, which included singing and shouting very loudly during his lucid dreams to see whether or not this activity translated to his physical body in order to wake his wife.

At the same time that Van Eeden was doing his experiments on lucid dreaming, a young Hugh Calloway was also experimenting with lucid dreams on his own. Calloway, better known to the magickal communities by his pen name Oliver Fox, called his lucid dreams "dreams of knowledge," because the dreams presented the knowledge that he was dreaming.

Carlos Castaneda introduced the modern American metaphysical community to the notion of lucid dreams in his 1972 publication *Journey to Ixtlan*. Through the character of the Yaqui sorcerer, Don Juan, Castaneda suggests that individuals seeking to achieve lucidity in their dreams should focus on their hands. Picking any predetermined object to focus on in dreams can help the dreamer achieve lucidity, but for Don Juan, hands were especially useful because "they'll always be there."

LUCID LAB WORK

The reality of lucid dreams was long doubted by scientists. However, with the development of REM sleep monitoring systems, it has become possible to track lucid dreams. Typically, the lucid dreamer agrees upon a pattern of eye movements that will signal the start of a lucid dream. With the lucid dreamer hooked up to REM monitors as well as an EEG—a device that monitors brainwave patterns—scientists in a laboratory setting can prove that the lucid dreamer is fully asleep, fully dreaming, and yet aware enough to transmit the prearranged sign.

Stephen LaBerge, a psychologist at the Stanford University Sleep Research Center is the recognized expert on lucid dreaming. Not only has he written the most modern and up-to-date book on the technique, but he has also developed a device for encouraging lucid dreams.

In addition to his gadgets, LaBerge is the originator of the MILD technique, or "Mnemonic Induction of Lucid Dreams." To use this technique, you wake yourself up from the dream and then immediately visualize yourself back in the dream. As you intentionally place yourself back in the dream, you remind yourself that the next time you dream, you want to recognize the fact that you are dreaming.

Mnemonic techniques seem to work best for inducing lucid dreams. Robert Monroe, who established himself with out-of-body experiences, taught a similar technique at the Monroe Institute in North Carolina. Monroe's technique also harnesses mnemonic repetition. Monroe suggests that, every time you go through a doorway, you should touch the threshold and ask, "Am I dreaming?" You should then look around at your environment, studying the people and objects around you to determine whether or not you are asleep. As the weeks pass, this activity will become such a habit that you will literally do it in your sleep. At some point, you will pass through a door, touch the threshold, and answer, "I am dreaming." Once this awareness has been achieved, you can lucid dream.

One of the misconceptions about lucid dreams is that they always involve total control of the dream environment. This simply isn't so. There are varying degrees of lucidity that we can achieve in our dreams, and sometimes it's easy for our lucidity to slip away in the dream. In fullest lucidity, you can shape the dream in almost any manner you wish, changing elements, adding people, and interacting with your environment in creative ways. Many people who lucid dream, myself included, use this level of control to fly in their dreams. When your level of lucidity is not as complete, you may be aware that you are dreaming, but you won't be able to exercise complete control over every aspect of the dream. For example, you might achieve enough lucidity to make the monster chasing you go away, but you might not be able to remove yourself completely from the rest of the dream. Not only does the level of lucidity achieved vary from person to person, it can also vary in each instance of dreaming. It takes a lot of practice and control to willingly lucid dream each and every time that you want to.

THE EYE OF THE TORNADO

Pearl was the first person I ever encountered who actively tried to lucid dream. We talked about our dreams a lot when we were in school together, sometimes passing notes about them written in secret code — a code which I remember to this day. Before I met Pearl, I had experienced lucid dreams, but I had never intentionally inspired them in myself. Several of these dreams involved flying. One of them, however, made me want to be able to recapture the experience and learn how to control it.

I was nine, and I was dreaming of a place I had never been. It was dark out, but somehow I could see as if it were twilight. There was a terrible storm, and I could see the clouds doing things that made them look like they were boiling in the sky. At first, I was watching everything from inside of a house. I was near a big bay window, and when the tornado came, it shattered the glass and started sucking things out into the yard. I was in a nightie, and I could feel the wind sucking and pulling at me. Debris whipped past me, and I could feel broken glass pelting my skin. I screamed, fighting not to get dragged out the broken window by the force of the wind. Somewhere in the middle of my struggles, I realized I was dreaming.

Immediately my perspective changed. The storm was still raging around me, but now I felt like I was hanging in the middle of the air. I was no longer directly involved in the action, but instead I watched things happen around me. I could see the house I had been in being torn apart by the wind. My perspective changed, and I was someplace else, but still watching the storm. This was a trailer park, and the storm was wreaking havoc with these tiny, fragile homes. My perspective shifted two or three times more, each time zeroing in on some new aspect of the destruction. I remember waking up with my heart in my throat. I looked at the clock and eventually I fell back to sleep. The next day, the newspapers told of a series of tornados that had hit in another state. The tornadoes hit around the time that I was dreaming. One of the photos in the newspaper showed the wreckage of a trailer park, and it looked eerily familiar. I had watched that destruction happen in the dream.

Dreams that foretold the future were not new to me. But the awareness that it *was* a dream was new, as was the strange ability to willfully move from place to place, exploring the full extent of the vision. I asked Pearl to teach me how to lucid dream partly so I could learn how to have such dreams at will. Of course, in her usual blunt manner, Pearl's advice for learning how to lucid dream was, "You just do it." While I've found that that is a valid suggestion, it didn't seem very helpful to me at the time. I never did learn how to willfully dream the future. I've learned that premonitions are much trickier than ordinary dreams. However, in the intervening years, I have picked up a few tricks that amount to more than "Just do it." Here are a few methods that work for me:

RECAPTURING THE DREAM:

When you wake up from a particularly interesting or vivid dream, don't try to shake off the sense of being asleep. Instead, keep your eyes closed and lay just where you are, holding onto the way your body felt as you were emerging from the dream. Likewise, hold onto the lingering mental and emotional sensations of the dream. Go over the dream in your mind, replaying it in as much detail as you are able. Let go of any sense that you are awake and instead let yourself consciously dream. Replay the entire dream in your mind, and when you get to the end, add to it. Keep in the exact style and feel of the dream. Continue any actions that might have been interrupted when you emerged from sleep. If you start to doze off while doing this, don't fight it. There is a very strong chance that when you fall back asleep, you will pick up where you left off in the dream. This time, however, you are likely to be lucid in the dream.

SUBCONSCIOUS PROGRAMMING:

As you are going to sleep, think about dreams and dreaming. Focus on your desire to lucid dream, and if you have a particular kind of dream in mind, think about that dream. Take a few moments to run through the major elements of this dream in your mind. Then think to yourself over and over, "Tonight I will lucid dream. Tonight I will lucid dream." Repeat this as you begin to fall asleep, until it is almost impossible to focus on the individual words. When you are too sleepy to really focus on the words, keep the intent focused in your mind. Do this for several nights running. This method will not work immediately, but it can work over time. Repeating your intent over and over again in your mind is a sort of self-hypnosis, and eventually, your subconscious will get the hint.

A PRAYER FOR THE DREAM KING:

Some people are not good at affirmations. For whatever reason, telling themselves that they're going to do something just doesn't sink in. Sometimes it's because they don't really believe that they can accomplish the task in question, and sometimes they just don't believe that affirmations can work. For some, there is a way to circumvent such doubt: calling on a higher power. A higher power can be anything that you believe is better and more capable than you. It can be a god. It can be a personification of your own Higher Self. It can even be a relative that you always trusted and looked up to, who's passed on and become an Ancestor.

Higher powers do not have to be objectively real to have power. Their power is your belief in them, and as long as you can forget that long enough to really believe, then you can call on them for help. At the beginning of this book, there is a prayer to the Dream King. The Dream King, as I explained in the previous chapter, is a fictional personification of the realm of dreams, but his fictional qualities make him no less the lord and master of the Dreaming. The fact that he is a character who appears in myths and stories automatically makes him larger than life. If you feel kind of silly telling yourself repeatedly, "I want to lucid dream," ask a higher power to help you. Try something like, "Dream King, Dream King, help me lucid dream tonight." Repeat it several times as you are falling asleep, making a real effort to reach out and connect with the personified Power that governs dreams. You may be surprised by the results.

THE BUDDY SYSTEM:

This technique, as the name implies, requires the help of a friend. This should not just be any friend, but someone very close to you that you trust. You need to be comfortable enough with this person to let them near you while you sleep. For some people, that's more comfortable than they get around anyone.

The technique is based on some of the same principles that are used in sleep laboratories to study dreams and dreaming. Put simply, when you go to sleep, you cease to be conscious of the world around you. However, your senses continue to take in information, and there is a kind of subconscious monitoring system that keeps track of this constant stream of input. If any noise or other disturbance in your environment moves past a certain threshold, you wake up. A lot of senses never move past this threshold, but on some level, you are still processing that information. Sensory input that comes just shy of crossing your threshold of awareness often gets translated into your dreams. If you have ever dreamt about a foghorn blaring only to wake and realize that your alarm has been going off for the past five minutes, you have experienced this effect. In sleep labs, it is used sometimes to steer the content of people's dreams and sometimes to guide them toward a lucid state.

In the buddy technique, you have a friend watch over you as you are sleeping. When it appears that you begin to dream (REM being a big tip-off), your friend should start, very quietly, to say: *[Name], you are dreaming. You know you are dreaming. [Name], you are dreaming. You know you are dreaming.* Your buddy should say this over and over again, starting out very softly and gradually getting louder. When it seems as if the words are almost loud enough to wake you, your buddy should get just a touch quieter and keep repeating this reminder for the duration of your dream. When the dream has past and all Rapid Eye Movement has ceased, your friend should wake you up and ask you about your dream.

This is not a one-time exercise but is something you should do over the duration of a full sleep cycle. Ideally, you should do it for several nights. The problem with this, of course, is that many of us lead busy lives, and waking up repeatedly in the night to tell someone whether or not we've been lucid dreaming is hardly restful. That's to say nothing of the time invested by your friend who agrees to the rather mind-numbing task of watching someone snore and wiggle their eyes beneath their lids. If you have a serious interest in dreams and dreaming, you can set a weekend aside to play around with this technique. Out of courtesy for your friend, you should return the favor, taking your turn as watcher of dreams.

DREAMING MACHINES:

Several machines are out on the market that can essentially perform the buddy technique for you. Stephen LaBerge has a lucid dreaming device that looks like a pair of space-age goggles. He wears them to sleep, and they monitor his eyes for signs of REM. When REM is detected, soft red lights go on in the goggles. The lights are not bright enough to wake him. Rather, they are just on the threshold of awareness, rousing consciousness just enough so he can become lucid in the dream. Robert Monroe patented something he called Hemi-Sync. This technique uses specially balanced and synchronized sounds that engage both the right brain and the left brain equally. These are combined with instructional tapes that lead the dreamer to a state of lucid dream. I have never personally tested either of these machines, so I cannot endorse them in any way. However, they are part of the technology that exists in response to people's quest to lucid dream. As observed throughout this book, different things work for different people, and you can only learn what does and doesn't work for you by trying things for yourself.

CHAPTER NINE

INVADING THE DREAMSPACE

You are lying in bed, trying to sleep, when suddenly you feel a presence in your room. You snap awake and try to sit up in order to see the intruder, but you discover that you can't move. A tingling feeling begins to wash over you, coming in waves. It's not entirely unpleasant. Under different circumstances, you might find it relaxing, but the fact that you can't move has you panicked.

You feel your heart pounding in your chest as you try to struggle, but it's as if some great weight is pressing you into the bed. You seem to see shadows moving out of the corner of your eye, and that sense that you are not alone increases. Instinctively, you know the intruder is somehow connected to the pressure, the tingling, and the inexplicable paralysis. You want to scream, but you cannot. Minutes go by, but they seem like hours. It becomes so hard to struggle because the pressure is making you feel weak and exhausted. It's almost a shock when you discover that you can move again. The intruder has withdrawn, as mysteriously as it came. By then you feel exhausted to the very core of your being. The next morning, you feel tired, achy, and, on some level, violated.

The experience outlined above describes a typical night terror. Sometimes known as Hag attacks, night terrors were once thought to be inspired by the visitation of an evil spirit. Our very word "nightmare" is connected to the tradition of the Hag attack. Another word for the evil spirit believed to inspire these terrible dreams is the Mara.

Currently, night terrors are believed to arise from hallucinations experienced at the threshold of sleep. French neurosurgeon Michel Jouvet discovered that the brain stem initiates a paralysis at the onset of REM. This serves to prevent us from getting up and physically acting out our dreams in our sleep. Typically, this paralysis ends once an individual emerges from REM sleep. The sense of paralysis that is a hallmark of the night terror is thought to result from a glitch in the system, so the individual becomes conscious before the paralysis has completely worn off.

Although sleep paralysis and hallucinatory states probably account for many night terrors, the above passage could just as easily be a description of a classic, nightly psychic attack. One of the reasons it's important to only dreamwalk to people with their consent is that uninvited dreamwalking can seem terribly invasive. What's more, dreamwalking can be used to intentionally invade someone's dreamspace and engage in psychic attack.

Let's face it. If you're really good at this technique and have a talent for shaping the dreamspace, you can dreamwalk to someone, put them through the mother of all nightmares, then zip safely back to your dreaming chamber in an hour or less. At the very least, you've interrupted your victim's rest and probably wrecked their nerves for the rest of the night. If you're really sly about it and simply build the nightmare from the target person's own dreams, the victim may never be able to identify the experience as a willful attack. Certainly, because it's "just a dream," even if your involvement is suspected, what can the victim really do?

SLAMMING THE DOOR

Earlier in this book, we discussed the idea of the dreamspace being a real "place." Although it might only be a cognitive space, a collection of images constructed by our individual and collective minds, it nevertheless acts like a real place. In addition to the curious properties of the dreamspace, there have been numerous comparisons between astrally projected individuals and ghosts. We have established that dreamwalking isn't exactly astral projection, but the two techniques definitely share some common ground. A significant patch of this shared territory involves the act of projection itself. Although astral bodies are not overtly involved, dreamwalking is nevertheless a variety of projection. A nonphysical aspect of self is sent out beyond the limits of the physical body. More often than not, this nonphysical aspect is only perceived in dreams. However, Casey had no trouble at all identifying me as I dreamwalked into his room.

Is the aspect that we dreamwalk with an astral body in the classic sense? I'm inclined to say no. However, under certain circumstances it is perceptible to others. If we accept that the dreamspace is, on some level, a real place, then we have to also accept that the portion of ourselves that walks there is also, on some level, real. If it is real in the dreamspace, on the rare times that it wanders out of that very specialized space, it is still real.

When we send ourselves out to dreamwalk, we occasionally also interact with the physical world. Whatever part of our nonphysical selves this aspect might be, it functions like a ghost. When it is interacting with something in the physical world, it can be perceived like a ghost. And if it looks like a duck, and it quacks like a duck . . . then it can be battled magickally like any other unwanted and invasive ghost.

If our dreamwalking selves function like ghosts, then we have to accept that dreamwalking involves a little bit of risk. Sufficient Will can conquer quite a lot of things, but a mountain of defenses can eventually erode one's desire to continue the battle, even if it fails to overcome one's Will. Approached as a spirit, a dreamwalker can very easily be kept at bay. Wards, shields, and other techniques can help protect individuals who have been targeted for an invasive dreamwalk.

The only thing that might counteract this on the attacker's side are deeply established, emotional links. Most people who engage in psychic attack do not pick random targets. Premeditated psychic attacks are almost always personal. In nearly all cases, the victim knows the attacker, and in many cases, the attacker and victim were close prior to the circumstances leading up to the attack. Emotional connections are expressed metaphysically through energetic links. As we've seen earlier in this book, links are the easiest focus to follow when targeting a person for a dreamwalk. If someone is dreamwalking to attack another persona psychically, chances are, the attacker is using pre-established emotional links to focus on the victim. And as long as the target person, on some level, wants to be connected to the dreamwalker—even if this desire is purely subconscious—that person can sneak in through the links. The links are like an open invitation, a door that is left slightly ajar, just in case the desired party visits in the night.

No amount of warding in the world will keep a dreamwalker out if those links remain active, even on the most subliminal level. The only way to close that door is to resolve the emotional entanglement. If the person on the other end of the link can manage this, then the door doesn't simply slam shut: it ceases to exist.

UNWILLING INVADERS

While I was writing this book, a friend from Texas contacted me over the Internet with a dreamwalking quandary. He had recently noticed that he was dreamwalking at night. One of these dreamwalking experiences involved two people that he definitely did not want to be visiting in this way. He was close with both of them, but personal issues made it both impossible and undesirable to approach them for consent. The situation was complicated by the fact that my friend was a psychic vampire. Although he chose to meet his needs ethically during his waking hours, feeding only from willing donors, his need for energy was expressing itself once he fell asleep.

Psychic vampires are individuals who need to regularly and actively take in human vital energy in order to maintain their own mental, physical, and psychic well-being. Often, they need this energy because there is a breakdown in their own systems that affects the way they connect to or process energy. Psychic vampirism can be related to chronic illness, but in many cases, it is simply something a person is born with, like a propensity for diabetes. There are many people who vampirize energy without ever realizing it, and these are the psychic vampires you read about in books about psychic self-defense. Many more psychic vampires are aware of their condition, and they have taken steps to learn about it and take an empowered approach to what others might see as a handicap or curse.

Most psychic vampires, regardless of their personal ethics, are prone to unintentional dreamwalking. When a psychic vampire reaches a certain level of energetic need, a kind of survival instinct kicks in and the psychic vampire dreamwalks to feed. Typically, the psychic vampire will unconsciously target friends or loved ones, traveling to them in dreams in order to take the vital energy that they so desperately need.

Knowing some of my experiences with psychic vampirism and dreamwalking, my friend wanted to know how I had managed to stop myself from visiting people that had not given their consent. While I was certainly willing to give him tips for restricting his nightly sojourns, I also had to be honest with him. I've been working with my psychic vampirism for nearly two decades now, and I feel that I have developed a great deal of control. Even so, the power of the unconscious is such that there remain instances where I suddenly find myself with a friend in a dream that feels all too real. I have never managed to completely stop myself from spontaneously dreamwalking.

While it is nearly impossible to exert complete conscious control over our unconscious actions, especially in sleep, we are not slaves to our unconscious minds. There are techniques that one can use to train the unconscious and offer direction. None of these are foolproof, but practice over time will certainly increase your chance of success. For psychic vampires who, like my friend, concern themselves with ethics, these techniques are important to master.

SETTING YOUR LIMITS

The first step psychic vampires should take when they realize they may be dreamwalking to feed is to set up a feeding pool. Determine if you have people in your life who would be open to being dreamwalked to. Talk with these people and see if you can set up an open door policy with them. Put plainly, make them aware of the possibility that you might visit them to feed in dreams, and see whether or not they're all right with you showing up unannounced. Agree to call them as soon as you can after you recall a dreamwalk involving them. If they feel that you have visited them and you fail to call, make sure they feel comfortable contacting you to let you know that you dropped by. When you confirm a dreamwalk involving them, be certain to thank them and double-check to make sure that the open-door policy still stands.

Once you have two or three people who are open to the idea of you dreamwalking to them, begin to program yourself to focus on these people before anyone else. When you feel yourself slipping toward a level of need that might inspire spontaneous dreamwalks, spend a little time before you fall asleep each night concentrating on these people. Remind yourself that it is ok to visit them, but also reinforce the notion that it is not ok to visit anybody else. Try not to focus specifically on any other person. Just go over the list of names in your head, visualizing each person in turn and recognizing their open invitations.

Because you are dealing with an unconscious activity that will happen after you slip into sleep, you cannot guarantee that you will focus solely on these permitted targets. Certainly, the act of programming your subconscious to choose them first can help to enforce this even when you are dreamwalking spontaneously. However, the greater your need becomes, the more your subconscious mind is inclined to feed quickly and efficiently, and this does not always mean sticking to permissible targets.

In my friend's case, the issue was that he had very specific people that he did not want to go dreamwalking to. In certain ways, preventing yourself from targeting someone is easier than simply trying to establish a list of permissible targets. The next suggestion I offered to my friend was intended in part as a caveat against allowing personal ethics to outweigh personal well-being.

NIGHTS IN THE DREAM CAGE

It is not possible to prevent yourself from dreamwalking entirely. However, it is possible to prevent yourself from being able to go anywhere. This approach is an extreme one, and it's certainly not pleasant for the dreamwalker.

I hit upon what I call the "cage technique" during a summer of difficulties, when I was so occupied with personal matters that my control over my energetic needs began slipping. I found myself dreamwalking repeatedly each time I slept. My targets were many and varied, and my interactions with them in the dreamspace were sometimes extreme.

As an active proponent of ethical feeding, this behavior was somewhat demoralizing to me, especially since no amount of control I tried exerting seemed to stop my nightly predations. Things reached a breaking point when I remembered a particularly intense feeding incident that occurred in the early hours one summer morning. Later that day, the friend that I remembered visiting called to complain about a terrible psychic attack she had suffered. She wanted me to come over and examine the bruising that had been left behind, in part to document it. She described the person she remembered encountering in her dream, and yet she could not equate this person with me because of the violence of the attack.

That drew a line in the sand for me. I was going to put an end to the dreamwalking however I could. Because I knew that the dream-self that was projected during dreamwalking often acted much like a ghost, I called a friend and had him set up wards throughout my room. Over the course of that afternoon, we turned my dreaming chamber into a spiritual prison, reinforcing the floor, the ceiling, the walls, all with the intent of keeping me in.

This method worked, but at great cost to me. When next I lay down to sleep, I dreamwalked as usual—but my recollection of the event was filled with shadowy visions of my room and the frantic sensation of scrabbling against door, windows, and walls, seeking for a way out. I awoke shaken and exhausted. Three nights of this experience was enough to convince me to look for a better way.

BETTER MOUSETRAPS

One of the things about feeding unintentionally in the dreamspace is that you almost always know the people you are dreamwalking to. I knew the people I had been targeting, and, unlike my Texan friend, I could speak to them about the matter. This made my task a fairly simple one. First, I suggested that my targets place dreamcatchers over their beds. The dreamcatcher is a Native American item that resembles a spider web woven within a hoop of wood. Often, it has a single stone, bead, or crystal caught somewhere within the web.

The dreamcatcher is a gift of Grandmother Spider, and it is supposed to catch bad dreams in its web, while allowing good dreams to pass through. By harnessing the imagery of the dreamcatcher and charging the item with intent, an individual can create a potent physical ward against unwanted nightly visitations. Dreamcatchers are made with the idea that some bad dreams are brought about by spirits, and so they could feasibly "catch" unwanted dreamwalkers as well, sending them back home.

Next, I instructed all of my targets to ward their bedrooms as I had done, only with the intention of keeping spirits out. Wards are essentially constructs of energy that one builds into existing walls, windows, and even doors. Warding a room can shield it from a variety of things, from spirits of the human dead to undesirable currents of energy, and even spirits of the living. Typically, the person erecting the ward has a specific intent in mind and usually speaks this intent out loud while projecting a barrier of energy into the wall to build the ward. All walls, windows, and other openings into the room are treated, as well as the floor and the ceiling. Some people like to also ward reflective surfaces, such as mirrors, on the notion that mirrors can sometimes serve as portals for spirits, if circumstances are just right.

You can erect a general ward in a room, something that's just intended to keep anything "bad" out, or you can have a very specific list of people and things that you erect a ward against. Sometimes having a physical symbol for a ward, such as a sigil you scribe upon the wall with your finger or a small charm you hang over the doors and windows can help focus your intent and build a better ward. One thing to remember about wards, however, is that their energy is not permanent. It's a good idea to reinforce wards on a room or house every month or so. If, for some reason, you experience exceptionally intense spiritual activity in the warded location, you may consider reinforcing the wards every few weeks.

Obviously, my friend in Texas couldn't approach people and tell them to buy dreamcatchers and erect wards. Part of his dilemma was that he could not approach the people he was unconsciously targeting. After thinking about the problem for a while, I suggested that he try shielding the people themselves. Shielding works pretty much like warding, but the focus is people. Most often, magickal workers concentrate on shielding themselves, but it's not unheard of to set up shields for other people, especially if they're in harmful situations and might not be able to shield for themselves.

In shielding, you simply visualize a barrier of energy that completely encompasses the person in question, like a bubble. Shields, like wards, can be constructed with specific goals in mind, and typically they are built to allow desirable energy through from both directions. Shields, like wards, also need to be reinforced every now and then, as the energy will degrade over time.

Because he was shielding people without their knowledge or permission, I warned my friend that he would have to be very specific to shield them only against himself. Anything else could be seen as invasive.

As well-intentioned as some efforts might be, even shielding a person against their will, under the wrong circumstances, can be interpreted as an attack.

My other recommendation to my friend was a reverse of the feeding pool programming. Before he fell asleep each night, he should focus on the two people in question, telling himself that it was not acceptable to dreamwalk to them. Reinforcing this repeatedly would serve to program his unconscious, passing the interdiction from his waking hours to his dreams.

PROTECTING YOURSELF

All of the protective measures outlined above can be used by people who feel that they are the targets of uninvited dreamwalkers—psychic vampires or otherwise. Shielding, especially, is much easier when done for yourself, and you can get very detailed in the precise nature and form of your shields. If dreamcatchers don't appeal to you, there are several other physical methods you can employ to help focus your barrier against unwanted dreams. I know one witch who draws a circle of sea salt around her bed to keep out invasive spirits. Similarly, author Colin Wilson was told by an English witch that erecting a pentagram beneath the bed would achieve the same result.

For those of a more whimsical bent, try designating a favored stuffed animal as your official "dream guardian." Imagine that the toy has a spirit and a personality, and that its sole purpose in life is to protect you from bad dreams. Build the construct up in the toy over successive nights, shaping it with energy and intent. Naming the toy can also help solidify the construct. You may even want to make a little sword of wood or foil-covered cardboard. Fix this to the toy's hand so it can fight off invasive dreamwalkers.

One of the beautiful things about magick is that it's powered by imagination. The more engaging and personally meaningful you make a technique, the better it will serve as a focus for your energy and your intent.

CHAPTER TEN

SEX IN THE DREAMSPACE

IT CAN BE FUN TO JOKE ABOUT Dr. Sigmund Freud's apparent obsession with sex. When every stick or serpent in a dream becomes a phallic symbol, it can seem a bit much. However, there is no denying that we are sexual creatures. The urge for sex is scribed deeply upon the most primitive centers of our brains. As rational, thinking creatures, we make conscious decisions about our urges, but that doesn't mean the urges just go away.

In the medieval era, the beneficent incubus of Greek and Roman dreaming magick was turned into a demon. What's more, the incubus became a sexual demon, often paired with its female counterpart, the succubus. Incubi and succubi were believed to visit good Christians in their sleep, tempting them into erotic experiences. These night-demons seemed to have a special affinity for holy men and women, appearing to nuns and priests more often than ordinary folk.

There is a very good reason for this phenomenon. In the medieval era, nuns and priests all took strict vows of celibacy. They promised not to act upon their natural sexual urges as demonstration of their love for god. Nuns, in fact, were known as Brides of Christ, because they were essentially betrothed to him when they took their office. The problem with sex, of course, is that our desires do not go away simply because we're ignoring them. Instead, when our sexual impulses have no out-let in our ordinary lives, they go underground, so to speak, to the realm of the subconscious. As we have seen throughout this book, that realm is closely associated with the realm of dreams.

In the medieval era, holy men and women were dreaming of erotic encounters with demons because they had no way to release these urges during the day. The only devil at work, however, was the sub-conscious mind. Rationally, the decision to be celibate made sense, but it went against every instinct that had been hardwired into the human machine since our days with the monkeys. The subconscious mind is not so much about rational decisions. Instead, the subcon-scious recognizes desires and needs. No matter how many vows one may make, the desire for sex, on some level, remains. And so the sub-conscious conjured demon lovers in dreams to allow for a release of the tension that quite naturally built up during the day.

HIDDEN DESIRES

While you are unlikely to be visited by demons in your sleep these days, the rules of the subconscious still hold true. Desires that are repressed through rational decisions don't simply go away. Do you find yourself attracted to your best friend's partner? Unless you have a very special relationship with your best friend, you can't exactly act on this attraction. Although your conscious mind enforces the proper behav-ior during the day, the attraction remains. Your subconscious mind then takes free reign with the attraction at night, playing out all man-ner of vivid scenarios in your dreams.

Most people never have to worry about their nightly affairs becom-ing public knowledge. What you dream at night harms no one, except maybe you. However, these rules change once dreamwalking comes into play. If you accept that when dreamwalking you are, on some level, having an actual interaction with the person you have dreamwalked to, subconscious urges can become problematic. Suddenly, you dream of having sex with your best friend's partner, and the next day, you're both having trouble meeting one another's eyes.

Spontaneous dreamwalking experiences are often initiated directly by subconscious urges. Our three most primal urges are the needs for survival, food, and sex. It is unsurprising, then, that these three potent instincts often lie at the heart of spontaneous dreamwalking experiences. Consider the countless records of crisis dreams. Many of these are instances of spontaneous dreamwalks, brought about through an overwhelming need to reach out and communicate with another human being. For psychic vampires, when a fundamental need like feeding is not being met, the subconscious takes over, seeking out a suitable feeding partner through the dreamspace. People who are dying reach out to loved ones in a last attempt to affirm their lives. And, although it may not be as widely talked about, there is a third sort of "crisis" that can inspire spontaneous dreamwalks: the need for sex.

It is possible—and actually quite common—to have sex in the dreamspace. Frequently, this manifests in cases of spontaneous dreamwalking, where our conscious minds have the least amount of control over what ends up going on. Obviously, sex in the dreamspace does not involve physical intercourse, although very graphic interactions can be acted out in dreams. Even though this is only dream sex, the sense of connection with another person and the resulting emotional entanglement remain the same. The subconscious pays little mind to the rules of propriety. In fact, it tends to run roughshod over all of the artificial boundaries that are so important to us in the waking world. Established relationships, boundaries of orientation and gender, concepts of chastity and fidelity all go by the wayside when the subconscious is in pursuit of its desires. When both parties remember the events of the night before, this can create some very uncomfortable situations.

Perhaps one of the most traumatic aspects of sex and dreamwalking is that it will often happen with people that you would never approach sexually in your waking life. This is where the tricky part of the subconscious comes into play. Having an attraction for someone that rationally you cannot act upon is bad enough, but sometimes there are attractions that you cannot even admit to yourself. These are held for safekeeping somewhere deep in the subconscious, and once you fall asleep, they can emerge.

Another factor in dream sex is the symbolic language spoken by the subconscious. Literal activities may not be presented as such in the realm of dreams. This holds true to some extent in all cases of dreamwalking, but it is especially true for spontaneous dreamwalks. It is important to remember that although, on some level, the interaction experienced in dreamwalking is real, it is nevertheless happening in the realm of dreams. No matter how lucid one might remain, certain rules of the dreamtime still apply. Lucidity may allow you to exercise some conscious control over what you do, but it is easy to get caught up in the unique logic of dreams.

According to psychoanalysis, dream symbols are developed through our personal experiences and, if Jung's concept of the collective unconscious holds true, influenced also by the archetypal experiences of humanity. What is the most potent symbol of an interaction between two people? Sex. Another meaning of the word "intercourse" is to have a conversation, to interact. Based on the research of Freud and many others, our dreaming minds love such plays on words, so that a simple conversation may manifest as something much racier within the boundaries of dream.

All of this holds especially true for psychic vampires who feed by dreamwalking. Feeding, no matter how politically correct we may seek to be, is already an erotic act. Publicly, the eroticism and sensuality inherent in the vampiric act is often downplayed, largely in an attempt to distinguish between real vampires who have an honest energetic need and vampire fetishists—individuals who get a sexual thrill from role-playing the part of the vampire in erotic encounters. No matter how physically chaste psychic vampires seek to be, the act of connecting to and withdrawing another person's energy is deeply personal, intimate, and sexually charged.

Feeding does not have to lead to sex, and quite often it does not. The details of an exchange are a matter of choice between consenting partners. However, the connection that is established energetically between two people during an exchange has potent corollaries to the connection achieved between two people having sex. The closeness, the elation, and the empathic rapport are all things that are natural by-products of the feeding act, and yet these are also some of the main things most people seek through sex. When we transfer this activity to the realm of dreams, the subconscious is not inclined to make petty distinctions. Feeding is about connecting with another person, and that connection culminates in an ecstatic exchange. In spontaneous dreamwalks, that connection is likely to become even more eroticized, and often it is symbolically represented through sexual acts.

BUILDING A BETTER BODY

Sex in the dreamspace, when undertaken responsibly, can be a very liberating experience. There are none of the concerns that go along with the physical body, such as the possibility of pregnancy or the transmission of disease. There is simply the ecstatic connection between two (or more) consenting adults. Since sex in the dreamspace takes place as the result of an energetic connection and not a physical one, it also lacks any kind of physical constraints. Essentially, you are limited only by your ability to imagine new expressions of how to achieve that incandescent release with your partner.

Depending on your tastes, you may choose to enjoy this interaction exactly as it occurs within the dreamspace: as an interaction of pure energy. This does not decrease the intimacy, nor does it decrease the ecstasy inspired by the act. For some people, these things are actually heightened when the burden of even an imagined body is left behind. However, other people may not want to pass up the opportunity to experience almost infinite sexual variety.

If you are capable of both dreamwalking and dreaming lucidly, consider how much you can control in the dreamspace simply by willing it to be so. You can change the landscape. You can defy the laws of gravity. You can gather your lover up in your arms and take flight to the stars. Another thing that you can change is the shape of your body. We touched upon this when we developed your basic eidolon. But, as you might have guessed, you are in no way limited to that simple representation of yourself in the dreamspace.

Once again, the possibilities are limited solely to your imagination. Have you ever wanted to change something about your physical appearance? What would you change if you could? You can make yourself thinner. You can make yourself stronger. You can lengthen your hair or smooth out the lines in your face. These are very simple changes. If you can enact one change on your eidolon, then you can enact quite a bit more.

One visualization that can help with this is the magick mirror. We used a simple version of this mirror when constructing the most basic manifestation of your eidolon. Now we'll do it again, with style. Put yourself in your dream haven. Call to mind the image of an ornate, full-length mirror. Focusing clearly on each detail of this mirror, craft its presence in your dream haven. Give the mirror its own special corner in your private portion of the dreamspace. Then spend some time standing in front of it. See yourself reflected clearly in the mirror. Examine every minute detail of your appearance.

As you regard yourself in this mirror, focus on one thing you'd like to change. Start with something simple. Change the color of your hair. Look at your reflection in the mirror and will your hair to change. As you did when first crafting your eidolon, it may help if you imagine yourself running your fingers through your hair. The change in color flows from your fingers wherever they pass. If you are not satisfied with the first result, change it again. All you have to do is want it, then make it happen. The changes in the mirror reflect the changes in your eidolon. Each time you make a change, run your hands along the area in question, seeing the change as a magickal effect that ripples from your fingers. If the change is a significant one, allow yourself to explore every new sensation that it opens up in you. Don't leave your place in front of the mirror until you have fully explored the change, experienced how different it makes you feel, and accepted it as how you will appear to others for the duration of this dreaming.

Once you master a simple change, try your hand at something more complex. Have you ever wanted to know what it would feel like to be the opposite sex? Some people do. If you can picture how you would like to look as a woman or as a man, you can conjure that image in the magick mirror and apply the change to your eidolon. Would you rather have slitted pupils or twin, curving horns? Once again, if you can imagine these things clearly enough so you can see them on your reflection, then you can craft these changes as part of your eidolon. As with simpler changes, take some time to really feel them, exploring everything they open up in you. If you like the changes, accept them and allow them to linger for the duration of the dreamwalk. If you are unhappy with something, by all means, change it!

Do you want to look like an angel? A demon? A unicorn? As long as you are able to continue to identify your consciousness with the image you see in the mirror, you can change yourself into whatever you want. Obviously, this can be applied to much more than just sexual games in the dreamspace. Shamans do something like this when they travel the dreamtime. Often, a shaman is given several different forms. Each form has a different set of strengths, and can be useful in different situations encountered in the dreamspace. You can use this ability to alter your form in a similar way, creating one or two alternate bodies that are better adapted or simply more comfortable for certain situations.

This kind of advanced shape-shifting in the dreamspace has a variety of magickal uses. However, for some people, the most rewarding use remains the opportunity to play out otherwise impossible fantasies. With a willing partner, there's no harm in it. Change your body to how you wish it could be, and enjoy that body in the dreamspace.

CHAPTER ELEVEN

LINES OF FLESH AND SPIRIT

IN ASTRAL TRAVEL, THE PRACTITIONER is always warned about the vulnerability of the silver cord. To cut that link between the astral body and the physical body is to bring about physical death—or so nearly all the authorities on the subject attest. But what about the dreamspace? Certainly we have seen that it is possible to wage psychic attacks against a target through dreamwalking. But how potent are these attacks? What kind of damage can really be done? Can dreamwalking have an impact on physical reality, such that psychic attacks might bring about actual, physical harm?

The notion that dream events can bleed over into physical reality lies at the heart of most dream magick. As I mentioned at the beginning of this book, in ancient Greece, "dormitories" were not found on college campuses—they were temples sacred to healing gods. A sick person, seeking a cure, would travel to the temple to go to sleep. It was believed that during this sleep, or "incubation," the god or daimon of the temple would appear in dreams to affect a cure. If the patient was not cured directly through the medium of the dream, the god or daimon typically gave instructions on the nature and cause of the disease, as well as tips for treating it in the waking world.

In modern folk belief, there is a lingering notion that if one dies in a dream, the physical body will die from shock. This has proven to be false, but given the vivid reality that many dreams seem to possess—at least during the course of the dream—it's hard to shake the idea that somehow, these flights of the mind can affect our waking bodies.

Certainly, the emotional events of dreams have physical repercussions. How many people have been pursued by some nightmare monster, only to wake up, heart pounding, lungs burning as if those last hundred meters had really been run? On the opposite side of things, how many people have dreamt of romantic encounters, only to awaken as their bodies responded very physically to the stimulus of the dream? In the medieval world, when any carnal pleasure outside of the marriage bed was viewed as a grave sin, people struggled to understand how and why their chastity could so easily be overthrown by a simple dream. As with many of the things that the medieval world did not understand, they assigned a demon to the phenomenon, the "incubus" described in the previous chapter. The word hearkens back to the incubation practices of the Greeks, where such night spirits were directly invited to enter the dreams of the sleeper.

Dreams are very real to our sleeping mind, and that perceived reality definitely translates over to our physical forms. Dreams can raise our blood pressure, trigger "fight or flight" responses, make our hearts pound, and even bring us to orgasm without any external stimulation. If it weren't for the paralysis that overcomes us when we dream, a phenomenon which sets in just prior to REM sleep, we would physically act out the contents of our dreams. Sleepwalking results from a partial breakdown of this natural paralysis, and classic night terrors are believed to occur when we accidentally achieve some level of waking consciousness before the paralysis has worn off. Certain individuals lack this paralysis response completely, and they are capable of doing great damage to themselves and to anyone sleeping with them. Completely unconsciously, they will get up in the night, fight, scream, and otherwise interact with physical reality as if it were the landscape of their dreams.

There is no doubt that dreams have some physical impact on us. However, most of that impact is internal, and it can easily be explained in terms of neurotransmitters and autonomous nerve response. However, autonomic nerve response can only explain so much. What about apparently metaphysical effects? If you wake from a nightmare with your heart pounding, that's one thing. But what if you dream of being choked only to wake and find bruises over your throat?

There are many ways we might attempt to rationalize such an experience. Perhaps you got the sheet wrapped around your throat at some point in the night. If this failed to wake you, it would be quite natural for the experience to manifest itself in a dream. Numerous experiments have shown how our sleeping minds are aware of stimuli in the physical world that surround us while we lie apparently insensible in sleep. Perhaps you hurt yourself at some point during the previous day. However, for some reason, you were oblivious to the fact at the time. Subliminally, however, your mind kept track of the wound and manifested your awareness of the damage in dreams. This, too, is a fairly common and well-proven experience. Our dreams exist, at least in part, for our subconscious minds to transmit relevant information to our consciousness—although, since they don't speak the same language, much of this information comes out as barely comprehensible imagery.

But what if it is none of these things? Can damage sustained in the dreamspace manifest physically? This is a highly debated topic, but numerous experiences reported by a variety of magickal practitioners suggest it is something we should explore.

DEMONS AND NIGHT TERRORS

Several years ago, I had a student whom we'll call "Doug." Doug felt that he had come under astral attack from some malevolent entity. This entity would dreamwalk to him and attack him within the dreamspace. Some of these attacks were so vivid and terrifying that Doug would crash awake, a scream struggling to escape his throat.

With the first few incidents, we of course considered the possibility that these nightly "attacks" might be nothing more than night terrors. When you believe in the possibility of dreamwalking, it can be tempting to assume that every dream and nightmare is some manner of communication, and that every denizen of your dreamworld has a real counterpart in the waking world. Especially before a student has cultivated the ability to distinguish between ordinary dreams and dreamwalking, this can be the case.

However, as the attacks continued, one night Doug saw the entity take the form of a huge bird of prey. It flew at him, beating him with its wings and clawing him with wicked talons. In the dream, he threw his arms up and tried to run, turning his back on this terrifying creature. Subsequently, it clawed his back to ribbons in the dream.

Upon waking, Doug's girlfriend discovered several bloody welts scattered across his back. They were about two inches in length and occurred in sets of three. These sets of parallel scratches covered his shoulders and middle back. There were perhaps six sets of them in all, and all seemed to have been made with the same object using a sweeping motion that went from the top of his body downward. It was not difficult to imagine the talons of a large bird making just such marks on someone who was trying to run from it.

What are we to make of this? There have been documented cases of people believed to be possessed or plagued by malevolent entities whose physical bodies bore evidence of what could only have been spiritual harm. In one account, documented by the famous ghosthunter Harry Price, onlookers watched as little Eleonore Zugun reacted as if scratched and bitten by an invisible tormentor. Moments after the child would react to the invisible attack, thick white welts and angry red teeth marks would appear on her body. In the American case that inspired William Blatty's *The Exorcist*, the young man believed to be possessed was repeatedly seen to be marked with scratches and welts, many of which spelled out words on his pale flesh. Bite marks, bruises, and bloody welts are not uncommon to such cases—but nearly all documented instances occur in the waking world.

Just about everyone knows the bit of folk wisdom that says if you die in your dreams, you will die in real life. The idea behind this is that things that occur in our dreamworlds can seem so real to our slumbering minds that our belief essentially enacts the event. This is psychosomatism taken to its logical extreme. However, this assertion, no matter how widespread, remains folk wisdom. It has never been proven to be real. As a good example, I've died in dreams several times, yet I'm here writing this, alive and well.

But anyone who practices magick knows that sometimes things from the invisible world can have a very real impact on the physical world. Can an attack in the dreamspace carry over to our physical bodies? Were Doug's scratches really the evidence of his nightly attacks?

Rationally, there are several possibilities that we have to consider before we accept that these scratches were truly physical manifestations of damage sustained in Doug's dreams. First, Doug was sharing his bed with his girlfriend, who I'll call Lisa. Lisa says that she was woken up when Doug started thrashing in his sleep. She was trying to comfort him when he came fully awake and it was shortly thereafter that she noticed the scratches on his back. When she asked him if he had scratched himself, he became even more agitated than before and rushed to the bathroom mirror.

Doug's fearful reaction to the presence of the scratches seems to suggest that he was not only unaware of them but that he was deeply shocked by their presence. But this does not guarantee that the scratches were a physical manifestation of events in his dream. First, we have to consider the possibility that Doug, in his restlessness, somehow inflicted the scratches on himself. It is one of the quirks of our dreaming minds that sensory input coming from our slumbering bodies can often be woven into the fabric of a dream. Even though we appear to be insensible to the world around us as we sleep, our subconscious minds do retain some awareness of the outside world. Music or other noises, including alarm clocks, are sometimes loud enough to penetrate the fabric of our dreams, but still not loud enough to rouse us from slumber. Physical sensations can also crossover, especially unpleasant ones. Anyone who's tried to sleep after surgery or with a newly broken bone will know how physical sensations can bleed over into dreams.

But what about Doug's scratches? Could he have somehow inflicted these upon himself, only to translate the pain into his dream? Their location, combined with the fact that he was sleeping on his back, suggests not, though the stronger argument against self-infliction would be the pattern and regularity of the scratches. Asleep and thrashing, Doug was highly unlikely to scratch himself six times repeatedly in exactly the same pattern of three parallel lines. Additionally, there is the sleep paralysis mentioned above. Typically, when we dream, our physical movements are curtailed, if not frozen entirely. This also argues against Doug's scratching himself in his sleep.

Could Doug's girlfriend have inflicted the scratches on him while he slept? This presupposes some serious treachery on her part, but when people are involved in metaphysical pursuits, unbalanced individuals have been known to make cries for attention by creating supposedly paranormal events. Skeptics have used this argument to successfully discount nearly every case of alleged possession in America since the 1930s.

If Doug's girlfriend was making such a cry for attention, she may be more likely to inflict the scratches on herself and carry on about psychic attack. However, in cases of Manchausen's disease, mothers who are needy of attention and validation have been known to wound and even poison their own children. Once the child falls ill from such treatment, the unbalanced parent then cares for the child relentlessly, gaining sympathy and admiration from friends and family for being so selfless in the face of apparent personal tragedy.

Attributing the qualities of Munchausen's disease to Doug's girlfriend seems a bit extreme. It is also hard to imagine that she sat up that night, leaning over him with a comb or even a fork, scoring his flesh while he slept. According to Occam's Razor, do we have to assume too much in order to pin responsibility on Lisa? Perhaps.

A more likely culprit might be Doug's cat. An affectionate creature, we can imagine that, sometime during the night, the cat crawled into bed between Doug and Lisa. Doug, caught up in nightmares as he had for the last several nights, thrashed and rolled over in his sleep. The cat became caught beneath him and, startled, the normally docile creature lashed out, trying to break free. The size and pattern of the scratches could easily be reproduced using a cat's forepaw, claws extended. Two considerations render this theory unlikely, however. The first, and weakest, of these concerns the angle of the scratches. All of the scratches were made from approximately the same direction. From shoulders to midback, the scratches seemed to come from about the same point above Doug's skin, sweeping downward. A cat, panicked and trapped under its owner in a bed, would have little interest in such regularity. Such an animal would be far more likely to produce a very chaotic pattern of scratches, some going top to bottom, some going left to right, and others slashing across diagonally. The second reason to rule out kitty's culpability is the simple fact that Lisa stated that the cat had been shut out of the bedroom.

All of this brings us right back to our original puzzle. Can an attack inflicted on someone's dream-self resonate through to the physical world with such force that it leaves actual, physical damage? In Doug's case, I never felt that there was enough evidence to be certain. There were simply too many variables to consider, and while the notion that Lisa inflicted the wounds for reasons known only to herself might seem a bit far-fetched, later events involving her rendered the entire incident suspect.

Another incident that I was directly involved in provides a clearer case.

THE VAMPIRE NEXT DOOR

From 1997 to 1999, I lived next door to an affable fellow I'll call Rob. Rob was a roofer by trade, in his late twenties, and, by all appearances, what one might impolitely label a "redneck." Rob watched WWF, held hockey tournaments on his Playstation, loved manly sports like NASCAR, and could drink with the best of them. That Rob and I ended up being fairly close friends seemed deeply unlikely, considering the cultural divide that existed between his laundry-strewn bachelor pad and my Gothed-out little apartment. And yet Rob was a great guy, and we frequently sat out on the balcony on cool fall evenings and warm summer nights alike, conversing about music, politics, and whatever else came to mind.

While Rob was well aware that I liked Sisters of Mercy just as much as Guns N' Roses and that I had a penchant for draping black velvet and lace over my windows, I was careful not to discuss my metaphysical practices with him. First of all, I had moved to this apartment in part to escape a neighborhood that had learned too much about me and my connections to vampirism. My former neighbors had not only been unaccepting of my beliefs, but many of them had also been openly antagonistic toward me because of those beliefs. I was determined not to endure the same kind of harassment in my new home.

Secondly, while Rob was great fun when discussing pop culture, current events, and even WWF (on the rare occasions that he got me to watch it) he really did not come across as the kind of guy who had any knowledge or interest in magick, let alone psychic vampirism. Rob was your standard all-American guy, grilling on weekends with a beer in his hand, working on weekdays through the sweat of his brow. "Mundane" was a word that fit him perfectly, and not in a derogatory sense. Utterly grounded in the physical world, he seemed infinitely at home in his torn jeans, T-shirts, and occasional loud, Hawaiian shirt. He had more videos and Playstation games in his apartment than books, and one of his prized possessions was a stuffed jackalope that looked morosely down from its place on the wall, two tattered plastic leis dangling from its stubby antlers.

Because I liked our friendship, I was not going to place it under undue strain by demanding that he accept things about me that lay so far outside of his world of beer and roofing as to practically reside on the planet Mars.

Rob would later prove to me two very important things. First, that my old neighbors had really been bigoted idiots whose close-mindedness was their problem, not mine. Second, that it was impossible to judge exactly what a person might understand about the world just based on the clothes they wore or the profession they pursued.

But for the moment, I still believed that a redneck roofer with a jackalope on his wall would balk at the notion of a vampire living next door.

As romantic as the vampire archetype has become in our culture, dealing with psychic vampirism is no picnic. When willing donors are scarce, a psychic vampire is faced with two options: commit an act of psychic attack by taking energy from someone without their permission, or starve.

1998 was a lean year for me. There were long periods of time where I simply did not have the resources available to meet my needs. Most psychic vampires who live outside of big cities like New York and Los Angeles, where awareness of and interest in the vampire subculture is fairly high, get used to bare, subsistence feeding. We can go out to clubs or other highly populated areas and take in the free-floating ambient energy that people in large groups naturally give off. This ambient energy can meet one's needs for a little while, but it's a delicate balance. The whole reason the word "vampire" is even appropriate for people like me is the fact that, in the end, to meet our needs, we must take energy directly from another human being.

To a certain extent, psychic vampires are always taking in energy. A psychic vampire can exert conscious control over this energetic intake, but it's not always easy. If, for some reason, the conscious, thinking mind is no longer in control, the subconscious default is restored. For psychic vampires, this means that once we go to sleep, if we are starving, we will seek out the energy we need regardless of our waking ethics. As I've described, this often results in bouts of spontaneous dreamwalking.

Energetic privation, dreamwalking, and my next-door neighbor Rob came together in a spectacular fashion one night in the fall of 1998. I still remember the encounter very vividly: I was in a neutral dreamscape when I became aware of traveling from this to some "place" else. I found myself in an unfamiliar dream. I stood as a spectator for a few moments, just acclimating myself to this foreign dream imagery. The shapes were indistinct, but I remember a lot of gold, like wherever I was lay drenched in sunlight.

I saw Rob in the dream, and it seemed perfectly natural to go to him and embrace him. He responded to this rather passionately, but rather than kiss him, I bent to his neck and, like a movie vampire, bit him. Even in the dreamscape, I am well aware that I feed on energy, not blood. So, despite the rather dramatic approach, there were no fangs, no pierced flesh, and none of the other traditional trappings. I could feel my teeth lightly clasping the skin at the base of his neck, just over the throbbing artery. I used his pulse as a focus to breathe in his energy. The motions and sensations were identical to my waking-world techniques for feeding from someone I'm intimately involved with. This level of familiarity with Rob, whom I considered a Platonic friend, stood out to me more than anything else in the dream.

At this point in my life, I was very familiar with the process of dreamwalking. I knew that it often happened unconsciously, especially when I needed to feed. I had been struggling to learn how to control this for several years, but it's practically impossible to exert conscious control over one's subconscious mind. The best I had been able to manage was some limited control over the pool of people I targeted in such nightly sojourns. These were close friends or fellow magickal workers that I had either exchanged energy with in the past or who had given me blanket permission for dreamwalking. Rob was an exception, and I was very surprised in the morning when I went back over the details of the dream.

While it's fairly easy to tell the difference between dreamwalking and regular dreams, I half entertained the hope that the experience had been nothing more than some unconscious wish fulfillment that expressed an attraction my waking mind was oblivious to. Judging by how much better I felt energetically upon waking, a part of me knew that the only wish fulfillment going on was my desperate hope that I had *not* fed from my mundane neighbor in my sleep.

It was normally my policy to contact the people I believed I had dreamwalked to. One of my reasons for this was simply to verify the experience. The secondary reason was to provide salve for my conscience and achieve permission after the fact or, if the person felt invaded, at least offer an apology. But what was I to do with Rob? The thought of even trying to bring the subject up made me queasy. I could already see the doubt in his eyes, could already hear him offering his opinion of my sanity.

And then, much to my surprise, Rob confronted me.

Afternoon rolled around and there was a knock on my door. When I opened it, there was Rob, looking both haggard and intense. He nodded by way of greeting and strode into my living room, pacing. He kept looking at me, then looking away. I had rarely seen him so agitated. Fear kept me from speaking.

"It's the strangest thing," he said after making several circuits of my living room. "I've never seen anything like it."

I watched him as he paced.

"I got up this morning and I kept trying to figure it out," he continued. "Where the heck did it come from?"

Though I suspected what he'd come over to discuss with me, I had no idea what he was ranting about.

"What's the matter?" I finally asked.

"A time-delay hickey," he stated flatly. "Have you ever heard of a time-delay hickey? I mean, that's all it could be, right? The last time I was with Lorrie was over a week. How does something like that show up after a week?"

"Time-delay hickey?" I wondered.

Rob continued to pace my living room like a caged tiger, every line of his body practically thrumming with nervous energy.

"Well, unless you know anything about it," he said. "I mean, you didn't have any weird *dreams* last night, did you?"

He pulled the collar of his T-shirt aside to reveal a round red mark at the base of his throat. It was in the exact same place where I had bitten him in the dream. The mark was identical to the marks that I often left on people after using that method to feed. Almost perfectly round, it's both like and unlike a hickey.

"Um . . . ." I said more than a few times.

"Yeah, I thought so," he said, fixing his eyes on me. "Care to have a talk with me?"

Oh boy.

We sat down. I was not comfortable having this conversation. My biggest issue, of course, was trying to explain not only psychic vampirism but also dreamwalking to someone I believed had no context for these things. But the mark was there, and we both obviously remembered the dream.

"You know, at first I thought maybe you'd just wandered into my apartment last night," Rob said. "Of course, you don't have keys. Me, I've climbed in through the balcony when I've locked myself out. But I can't see you climbing the balcony."

I admitted my lack of proficiency in the art of balcony climbing.

"So you weren't sleep walking," he concluded. "I was pretty much going to write it off as just a fun dream, and then I saw this thing. Most people don't get hickeys in a dream."

I pondered my hands for a few moments, nails rough from too much typing.

Finally, I asked, "So what if it was something more than a dream?"

"I figured that much out. You know," Rob said, lighting a cigarette, "you were looking pretty sickly the past few weeks, but today there's color in your cheeks."

My fingers were once more deeply interesting. I sighed and tore off one of the tattered nails.

"About that, Rob," I started, rolling the piece of nail into a tight little curlicue. "I'm not sure how to explain this. You said you've taken some martial arts, right?"

Rob smoked and nodded. Around the cigarette he said, "Tae Kwon Do, karate, yeah."

"So you know about that stuff called *chi*" I continued.

Rob nodded again, fidgeting with his cigarette pack.

"So some people have a lot of *chi* and some people don't have enough. There's things you have to do to balance it out."

I flicked the bit of nail onto the floor.

"Yin, yang, I get that," Rob replied a little impatiently. "I don't have half the books you got, but I've read the *Tao Te Ching*."

"Well, I don't exactly have enough *chi* and sometimes I need to take it. Usually only with permission," I added quickly. "But once in a while I slip."

I was staring at the floor, waiting for him to start telling me that I was deluded or crazy or worse. A lot of scenarios for his possible reaction had been playing themselves out on the insides of my eyes. None of them fit his actual response.

"So you're a psychic vampire," he laughed. "Why didn't you just say so?"

I stared at Rob for several moments, trying to remember how to work the muscles of my jaw.

"What?" I finally managed.

"You're a psychic vampire," he repeated. "What's the big deal? Or did you think I wouldn't know what that was?" He tapped ash from his cigarette, smirking. "I know a lot more than most people give me credit for. I might not have your education, and I might not look all serious and spooky, but that doesn't mean I'm ignorant."

Point taken, and at least a little faith in humanity restored.

A lot of the tension left the room after that, and we slipped into our old, easy-going conversation, delving into topics that had seemed taboo just hours before. Rob really did surprise me with his knowledge of the occult, and his matter-of-fact acceptance of what I was left me profoundly happy to be able to call him "friend."

I was still embarrassed about the dream, however. I wasn't entirely comfortable with the actual circumstances of the exchange, but I also knew that it wasn't unusual for feeding in the dreamspace to manifest as an erotic exchange. Was there sexual tension between Rob and myself? Only if we let ourselves take the action of the dream too seriously.

I also didn't like that I had left a mark, but I could come up with no other explanation for what Rob had on his neck. He would have had an identical rosette if I had actually walked into his room and embraced him as I did in the dream. But, as he himself had already pointed out, even if I had been sleepwalking as opposed to dreamwalking that night, I had no keys to his apartment. While my door was rarely locked, he had spent too many years in rough neighborhoods not to lock his own door. If we were really desperate to come up with a rational explanation for the mark, I suppose we could have concluded that we were both sleepwalking the night before, that he had unlocked the door for me, and processed the entire experience as a dream. Never mind that I had not gone sleepwalking since I was eight and Rob had never sleepwalked in his life.

Rob and I both believed that I left that mark in a dream. It would not be the only time that dreamwalking on my part left that kind of evidence. It taught me that the lines between sleeping and waking, physical and nonphysical, could be hazy indeed.

CAUTIONARY TALES

Magickal practitioners often walk a thin line between belief and gullibility. What we practice requires a certain amount of suspension of disbelief. After all, everything we encounter in our waking lives tells us that we cannot affect physical reality with just a thought. And yet this premise is the very basis of magick: *thought creates effect*.

Simply because we choose to accept that in some instances apparently unreal events can have real effects does not mean that we must abandon all reason. Not every stray thought creates a magickal effect, and not every dream is a dreamwalking experience. Can events in the dreamspace bleed over unexpectedly into physical reality? To a certain extent, the belief that they can defines the art of dreamwalking. And yet it is essential for any good magickal practitioner to cultivate a kind of open-minded skepticism.

When you have an experience that you believe is metaphysical in nature, consider all other possible explanations first. I've demonstrated a good way to go about this in both examples given above. Do not let your desire to believe in something otherworldly blind you to simple facts that provide a very real-world cause. Especially when dealing with the realm of dreams, we have to take care not to be overly credulous. Our minds are far more complicated than many of us imagine them to be, and based purely on physiology, they can bring about distinct physical effects that seem to have no connection with physical reality. Placebo effects, subliminal information, and psychosomatic illnesses all demonstrate just how profound an impact our minds can have upon our bodies. To a certain extent, much of magick is simply making use of these deeper aspects of our minds, and when it gets right down to it, whether you define this as magick or psychology is just a matter of personal belief.

Ultimately, you and you alone can judge the validity of your experiences. You should never surrender this right, but you should also not use it as an excuse to indulge in wish fulfillment. Make a thorough investigation of every experience and decide for yourself.

A BRIEF HISTORY OF DREAMS

Dreams have both fascinated and puzzled humanity for thousands of years. Artemidorus Daldianus, a physician who lived in the Rome of Antoninus Pius and Marcus Aurelius, believed that he was commissioned by Apollo himself to write a treatise on dream interpretation. The resulting five volume work was called *Oneirocritica*, or *The Interpretation of Dreams*. It was penned around the second century of the Common Era and was one of the most extensive early works in the Western world to take a systematic approach to the meaning of dreams. Artemidorus's *Oneirocritica*, reprinted in the sixteenth and seventeenth centuries in Europe, remains one of the primary sources for the meaning of dream symbolism outside of modern psychology.

Even before Artemidorus, however, dreams were a full-time occupation of the ancient world. From the temples of ancient Egypt to the tales of the Biblical Patriarchs, a lot of ink was spilled over the proper interpretation of dreams. Dreams had a mysterious potency for our ancestors because they were not believed to be mere fantasies that played through our minds at night. Dreams were seen as the primary method by which the gods communicated with mortal men. Dream incubation, the practice of sleeping in a ritually prepared space in order to make contact with gods in dreams, was practiced throughout the ancient world. In some cultures, like ancient Sumeria, the right to contact the gods through dreams was reserved for kings. In Egypt, Greece, and the Roman world, anyone who approached the dreamspace properly could be visited by a god or instructing daimon.

Oneiromancy was the ancient practice of telling the future through dreams. Related to the belief that the gods could communicate with mortals in their sleep, oneiromancy relied upon the notion that many different levels of reality intersected in the realm of dreams. Through dreaming, not only could mortals come into contact with spirits and gods, but they could also connect with the distant future and the distant past.

As times changed and empires fell, dreams became no less mysterious to our forebears. In medieval Europe, the spirit that was believed to inspire healing and prophesy during dream incubation was transformed from helpful genius to malicious demon. We know it now as the incubus, and all traces of its formerly benevolent identity have been lost.

This small detail offers a significant insight into how the spread of Christianity impacted the attitude on dreams and dreaming. In early Christian Europe, dreams still occupied that hazy place between the mortal and spirit worlds. However, such gray areas did not fare well in a culture that had adopted a starkly black-and-white worldview. The Bible taught that dreams could be prophetic visions granted by God, but only very special individuals were graced with such miracles. More often than not, the phantasmagoric images that haunted people at night were attributed to the Devil or his many minions sent to subvert the good people of the world. St. Jerome, writing in the fourth century C.E., deliberately mistranslated parts of the Bible to condemn the practice of observing dreams. In the face of such rigid thinking, there was little room for the interpretation of dreams.

The Renaissance saw a renewed interest in all aspects of the classical world. Wealthy families, like the Medici of Florence, financed the translation of a number of classical texts. Included in the more traditional Greek and Roman works on philosophy and history were several books on magick and spirits. The Church was not pleased by what it considered a scandalous Paganizing of European art and literature. But no matter how high Savonarola and other outspoken priests piled the bonfires of burned books, there was no denying that people's interests had once more turned to the gray areas of human experience. Notably, a new edition of Artemidorus's *Oneirocritica* emerged from Venice in the early 1500s.

From that time forward, the Western opinion on the significance and mechanism of dreams has wavered back and forth between potent meaning and utter meaninglessness. René Descartes, a seventeenth century French mathematician who is viewed as the father of modern philosophy, maintained that dreams were nothing more than fanciful images conjured up by an irrational portion of the mind. Even so, on the evening of November 10, 1619, Descartes had a series of dreams that inspired his life's work. Despite his belief in the irrational nature of dreams, Descartes himself maintained that these particular nighttime visions were so potent that they could only have come "from above."

In the Age of Reason and the Industrial Era, the official stance on the fanciful meaninglessness of dreams stood in stark contrast against the dream-inspired experiences of artists, composers, authors, and even military leaders. Coleridge's poem "Kubla Khan," Stevenson's *Dr. Jekyll and Mr. Hyde,* Mary Shelley's *Frankenstein,* and portions of Wagner's *Ring Cycle* were all conceived in dreams. Napoleon Bonaparte put such stock in his dreams that he based many of his military tactics upon them. At the Battle of Waterloo, he discounted a dream that foretold his defeat, dooming his empire.

In November of 1917, a young German corporal heeded a dream that foretold the shelling of his bunker. Wakened from his sleep by a nightmare of being buried alive, he wandered out to walk the night, only to have a heavy artillery shell completely destroy the bunker and everyone still sleeping within it a short while later. Nightmares may have continued to inspire him throughout his later life: the young corporal became known to the world as Adolf Hitler.

JUST A CIGAR

An Austrian Jew driven from his homeland by that selfsame German corporal essentially wrote the book on the modern approach to dreams. Sigmund Freud is remembered by the world as one of the fathers of modern psychology. In 1899, he published a landmark work, *The Interpretation of Dreams*—a title conspicuously reminiscent of Artemidorus's famous work. In many ways, Freud was styling himself as the Artemidorus of the twentieth century, attempting to redefine the modern approach to dreams. Freud was so intent that this work should pioneer dreams for a new era that he convinced his publisher to list the publication year not as 1899 but as 1900, so as to set the book firmly in the twentieth century.

The response to *The Interpretation of Dreams* was not immediately gratifying. It took eight years for Freud to sell six hundred copies of his book. Eventually, however, his ideas caught on, and they continue to influence how we view dreams today. Freud saw dreams as manifestations of repressed desires, often sexual in nature. This basic premise of *The Interpretation of Dreams* was founded on the notion that there are portions of the mind that are hidden to us that nevertheless act upon us—often beyond our conscious control. Freud had names for some of these secret selves: *Id, Ego, Superego.* These other selves or aspects of self do not generally communicate with us directly. However, communication does occur between these various layers of the mind. Most of this communication occurs in the form of symbol, and most of these symbols emerge in our sleep through dreams.

An accurate analysis of dream symbols, Freud maintained, would allow a trained psychiatrist to understand the hidden issues that lay beneath a patient's disturbed behaviors. Such insight could then be used to address the root issues at work in the patient's life, greatly speeding the process of therapy. The idea caught on, and psychoanalysis was born.

Working with some of the greatest minds in early twentieth-century psychology, Freud made pioneering steps in exploring the undiscovered country of the human subconscious. Additionally, he made dreams a subject of serious study once more. No more were dreams merely the meaningless products of an irrational mind, as Descartes and many other thinkers from the Age of Enlightenment had declared. Dreams instead spoke to us about those things we were not willing or able to say out loud in our waking hours. They were filled with complex images of things we wanted, but could not have.

Perhaps the one significant flaw in Freud's theory was his over-sexualization of imagery in dreams. If one dreamed of a snake, it represented a phallus. As far as Freud was concerned, church steeples, daggers, sticks, syringes, and practically any other long or pointed object that appeared in dreams represented the male sexual organ. Climbing a ladder was an image of heightening sexual excitement. Flying and even playing the piano in dreams were abstrusely connected with the rhythm of the sexual act. This near obsession has rendered the term "Freudian" synonymous with the notion of repressed sexual imagery. Given Freud's fascination with phallic symbols, it's interesting to note that the analytical Austrian was rarely seen without a large cigar in his mouth. Inquiries on the meaning of this elicited the quick response, "Sometimes a cigar is just a cigar."

LANDSCAPE OF MYTH

Freud did not see sex in each and every dream, but it was certainly a theme he returned to again and again. Carl Jung, a student of Freud's, eventually grew to believe that Freud's recurring focus on sex was causing him to overlook the deeper meaning of many dream symbols. In 1909, while traveling for a conference, Jung had a famous dream that ultimately severed his relationship with Freud. Jung dreamed of exploring a house—a symbol that Freud felt ubiquitously represented female sexuality. In the dream, Jung saw this house as his ancestral mansion, and he was exploring successive layers beneath this ancient building. He climbed ever deeper through older and older layers of the house until he reached a cave that seemed to date to the Stone Age.

It was Jung's opinion that the house represented his own mind. The first floor was his conscious mind—the part of the house he essentially lived in. The basement and successive layers beneath that, Jung felt, represented the vast territory of the uncon-scious that lurks beneath our conscious minds. As Jung probed ever deeper into the vast chambers below the main portion of the house, he encountered successively older layers of his psyche. When he reached the cave, he felt as if he stood at the very foundation of human experience, a place that lingered in the deepest shadows of our minds. To Jung, this cave represented the common point from which we all had come, a kind of communal mindspace.

Excited by the dream as well as by his analysis of its meaning, Jung wrote to Freud. Freud disagreed completely with Jung's analysis, insisting instead that the house represented a woman in Jung's life. Because Jung had discovered human bones deep within the foundations of the house, Freud determined that Jung was secretly harboring a wish to kill two of his female relatives. Freud pressed the issue, forever alienating Jung.

Jung came away from this dream with elements of two of the most important concepts he would develop in his psychiatric career. First, he felt the deepest layer of the basement, that shadowed cave that seemed to date to the Stone Age, represented not only the deepest portion of his own unconscious mind, but also a part of the unconscious mind shared by all humanity. It represented not only common origins physically, but common origins of a psychological nature as well. Jung saw this as a repository of all the mythic images shared by humanity worldwide, and he dubbed it the "collective unconscious."

Intimately connected to this notion of the collective unconscious was the idea that certain potent symbols lie at the core of each of us. Jung called them archetypes. These symbols have universal meaning, and that universal meaning is established by their shared origin in the collective unconscious. Jung supported his notion of archetypes through the dreams of many of his patients. Again and again, his patients would report images in dreams that accurately reflected symbols from ancient myths—myths that the patients had never formally been exposed to.

CLASSIFYING DREAMS

Deeply personal and often inscrutable, dreams nevertheless continue to fascinate us. No matter how surreal the images get, our nightly visions resonate with a profound sense of meaning that lingers always on the edge of understanding. Partly because of this tantalizing sense of deeper meaning, psychologists and neuroscientists have devoted millions of hours and dollars to researching the nature of dreams.

We have learned a little since the days of soothsayers and dream interpreters. Neuroscientists now believe that at least some dreams are involved in the transfer of information from short-term memory to long-term memory. This process is called memory consolidation. Memory consolidation explains why so many of our dreams are filled with a series of often disjointed images that echo our experiences from the day before. According to theories of dream consolidation, dreams are the stories our minds tell us as they try to make sense of all the varied bits of information being processed during what amounts to a memory dump. A related theory, developed in 1966 by Roffwarg, Musio, and Dement, suggests that REM sleep reinforces memory patterns by essentially exercising our neurons. Images and ideas connected to the information stored in those neurons are re-experienced as they fire in the form of dreams.

As compelling as the memory theories of dreaming can seem, they do not account for all dreams. Many dreams seem far too organized and meaningful to simply be stories built up around a data-processing function, and certainly not all dreams focus on specific clusters of memory. Some thematic dreams recur again and again among diverse people separated by time as well as distance. Dreams of flying, dreams of being caught naked in public, dreams of falling, and dreams of pursuit are all archetypal dreams that have been reported by sleepers from Kansas to Canton. These dreams seem less involved in processing raw data and more involved in transmitting a message from our subconscious minds to our consciousness. These message dreams give vivid expression to fears and anxieties we have failed to admit to ourselves. Sometimes, they tell us that the things we fear are not really as bad as we're making them out to be.

Such symbolic dreams have, for many years, been the focus of a branch of psychology called psychoanalysis. The imagery in these dreams is reviewed in terms of the dreamer's waking life, and cues are sought that reveal the source of undifferentiated anxieties, stress, and tension. Compellingly, the dreams themselves often provide the solution to the problem. This suggests that there is a part of the human mind that knows far more about our waking lives than we can ever consciously realize.

A third type of dream dovetails neatly with psychologically insightful messages from the subconscious. Many artists, writers, and scientists have experienced a dream that shed sudden and unexpected light upon what seemed to be an insoluble problem. These problem-solving dreams may arise from a combination of data processing and subconscious messaging. Essentially, as the individual dreams and reviews the material that has been the focus of so many waking hours, the subconscious takes note of some crucial piece of data that the conscious mind has consistently overlooked. This data is flagged and presented in some symbolic context that reveals how it answers the problem.

Thomas Alva Edison very consciously harnessed this subconscious effect. Whenever he was stumped about an invention, he would sleep on it, literally. Sitting in his chair, Edison would loosely hold two large ball bearings in his hands. Metal pans were placed strategically beneath him. When he fell deeply enough asleep, his hands would relax their grip on the ball bearings. The balls, in their turn, would drop into the metal pans, causing such a clatter that Edison would snap to full wakefulness. The brief sojourn that this allowed him to take to the realm of dreams almost always yielded some crucial insight to the problem at hand.

Some dreams seem neither concerned with data, messages, or problem solving. These dreams, vivid and engaging, tell us a story while we sleep. These are the dreams that will cast the dreamer as the main character in his or her own private nighttime movie. Filled with romance and high adventure, such story dreams seem to be conjured up for sheer entertainment. Many people have recurring entertainment dreams, experiencing them as if they were nighttime serials. It's not uncommon to dream one vivid installment and then pick up the story line in a subsequent dream months or even years later.

According to the research of Herman A. Watkin, introverted people tend to experience dreams like this more often, probably because their own internal landscape is already perceived as an acceptable source of private entertainment. Extroverts, on the whole, tend to experience less imaginative dreams. By Watkin's definition, this is because extroverts are "less differentiated" than introverts and rely more upon the outside world for their sense of identity. As a result, they are more inclined to seek their entertainment in the external world, rather than in dreams.

At this point, we have identified four distinct types of dreams:
- Memory Dreams, connected with information processing
- Messages from the subconscious
- Problem-solving dreams
- Story dreams, for entertainment

There is a fifth type of dream that is not as widely recognized by scientific authorities on dreams and dreaming. This is the paranormal dream. Paranormal dreams contain information that the dreamer could not have gained through ordinary means. Telepathic dreams, dreams of recently deceased loved ones, dreams of future events, and dreamwalking experiences all fall into this final category. Although paranormal dreams certainly fall on the fringes of accepted science, they are nevertheless so persistent and so widespread that they have repeatedly been the subject of scientific inquiry.

DREAM TELEPATHY

For several years in the 1940s, a strange debate was going on within the psychological community. It was dubbed the "Eisenbud-Pederson-Krag-Fodor-Ellis Controversy"—named for the main voices in professional psychiatry who were involved in the debate. It raged for years in the psychological journals in the form of studies and letters written by individuals from both sides of the debate. Eisenbud presented a scholarly analysis of psychic phenomenon that manifested during sessions of psychoanalysis, particularly in the content of multiple patients' dreams.

By this point in time, Freud had opened wide the doors to the realm of dream, and psychoanalysis was practiced widely by a diverse number of therapists. Certain strange qualities of psychoanalysis had already started to make themselves known. For one, it became quickly apparent that patients of Freudian psychoanalysts tended to dream in Freudian symbols, while patients of Jungian psychoanalysts obligingly dreamed in Jungian symbols. This was not merely a matter of the analyst imposing his or her own interpretations on the reported dream imagery, but actually involved a shift in the typical imagery of the patients' dreams during the course of therapy. Subconsciously, the patients seemed to be accommodating their analysts' views, possibly in an attempt to win their approval.

Many psychoanalysts had also begun to notice what Jan Ehrenwald referred to as "psychic leakage" between patient and therapist. This leakage seemed to occur more frequently when the doctor was experiencing issues that dovetailed with the patient's own needs and anxieties. Suddenly, the patient's dreams contained material pertinent to the analyst's own life. Often, the patient had no way of knowing this material, and yet in several instances, the material was too detailed to be coincidental. One patient dreamed that his analyst had stolen a soap dish when precisely that sort of soap dish had been mistakenly delivered to the doctor's home—and he had decided to keep it despite the fact that he did not pay for it. The doctor was feeling somewhat guilty about this decision and was still trying to rationalize it to himself when his patient reported the dream that more or less scolded him for the offense!

Three primary factors seemed to be at work in these telepathic dreams. First, there was usually some interest in dream telepathy on the part of the psychiatrist. Interestingly enough, this interest never had to be directly stated to the patient. As with patients of Freudian analysts dreaming in Freudian imagery, it was as if the patient unconsciously sensed the psychiatrist's interest and obliged by providing material that matched that interest. Secondly, the therapist exhibited some need in his or her personal life that dovetailed with the patient's own needs. And finally, connected to the second factor, there was anxiety on the part of the therapist that dovetailed with the patient's own anxieties.

The paper that sparked the Eisenbud-Pederson-Krag-Fodor-Ellis Controversy suggested that these dreams were legitimate instances of telepathic communication. Psychiatrists who criticized this view did not dispute the dreams themselves. Instead, it was suggested that the therapists reporting the dreams were giving unconscious cues and subliminal suggestions to their patients. The greatest criticism was leveled against the fact that psychiatrists who had a prior interest in ESP were more likely to have patients exhibit telepathic dreams. And yet, if the psychiatrists were coaching their patients from the couch, then many of them were doing so unintentionally. The majority of the dreams recorded as instances of telepathy contained details that were not only deeply private but also personally embarrassing to the therapist.

Extrasensory abilities were a hot topic in the early psychological community, and one's attitude toward them could make or break an analyst's career. Carl Jung is still widely derided for his belief in the paranormal, a belief that started very early in his career and influenced his work on concepts like synchronicity. Freud, on the other hand, toed the official line, at least publicly. At a lecture given in 1911, Freud addressed dreams and telepathy, largely debunking any real paranormal qualities to so-called psychic dreams. Like the third big name in psychoanalysis at the time, Alfred Adler, Freud insisted that the majority of supposedly psychic experiences were simply results of unconscious memory or subliminal perceptions—information that we had gathered unconsciously through our five ordinary senses and mistook for something we had no previous knowledge of.

And yet even Freud had his doubts. In a paper entitled "Psychoanalysis and Telepathy," Freud openly says, "It is probable that the study of occult phenomena will result in the admission that some of these phenomena are real." The paper, written in 1921, was never published in Freud's lifetime. It was not an isolated incident, however. A careful reading of Freud's work shows that he was a believer, despite his official stance of skepticism. In another bold statement, Freud observed that "sleep creates favorable conditions for telepathy."

This declaration became the core premise for a series of experiments run in the 1960s by a team of doctors at the Maimonides Medical Center in Brooklyn. Doctors Montague Ullman and Stanley Krippner devised extensive experiments to test the validity of Freud's observation. As both doctors report in the 1973 publication, *Dream Telepathy*, the experiments demonstrated that there is a definite psychic side to dreams. Given bold, visual images to focus upon, subjects were able to transmit key elements of these images to individuals who slept in isolation—sometimes many miles away! Members of the American Society for Psychical Research were already well aware of this fact. About two thirds of the spontaneous psychic experiences reported in the United States manifest in dreams.

DREAM STORMS

Dreams are funny things. Perhaps more than any other aspect of human experience, they can highlight the fact that we are all connected on some hard-to-define level. This fact was really driven home for me while writing this book. It all started the night of November 29, when I started the dreaming experiment. While I did not set out that night to do anything more than have some noteworthy dreams that would be fun to recount in my journal, I still ended up having an unusual dreamwalking experience. What's more, my call to the Dream King for interesting experiences was hardly limited to that one sleep cycle alone. For several weeks after that night, I had intensely vivid dreams. Spontaneous dreamwalking experiences abounded, as did several experiences that were very new to me. And after a little while, it became apparent that this rash of vivid dreaming was not limited just to me. It seemed as if my dreamwork was spilling over into the minds of my friends, many of whom had no idea I was working on this book.

The first to contact me about the dreams was Zamion, my *prasadi*, or primary donor. Zamion lives about two hours away from me in Columbus, Ohio. She knew I was working on a dreamwalking book, but she didn't know all the details about the book. She certainly didn't know that I started a dreaming experiment on November 29, and yet she called the next day because she needed to talk about some unusually vivid dreams she had experienced the night before. Over the course of the next few days, we both experienced exceptionally vivid dreams and while we did not share identical dreams, there were unmistakable themes that seemed to echo between us. Because of our relationship as vampire and donor, this was not too unusual. We had certainly shared space in one another's dreams before, and she had been the subject of a few dreamwalks. However, it was unusual for her to have so many vivid dreams, and the dreams continued over the space of many days, ever increasing in their complexity and strangeness.

Zamion's parallel dreaming was unusual enough, but another friend, this one living at a distance of 1300 miles, called unexpectedly with his own dreaming experience. He was more in the dark about the dreamwalking book than Zamion, and yet he had called me specifically because he felt he had just had his first dreamwalking experience. A skeptic who was only beginning to adjust to the notion that he might have some psychic abilities, the dreamwalking experience caught him completely off-guard. He was particularly concerned about the spontaneous nature of the dreamwalk because he had no way of asking the permission of the two people it had involved. When I asked him how the rest of his dreams had been over the past few weeks, I learned that he, too, had started dreaming very vividly around the start of my own dreaming experiments.

Zamion, now intrigued by the parallel nature of our dreaming, began keeping an eye out for blog entries our friends had made about their dreams. She noticed a definite increase in reports of dreams from the time of the experiment onward. Friends from all aspects of our extended network commented repeatedly in their online journals about the sudden increase in the instances and intensity of their dreaming. Even more interesting was the fact that many of these people related dreams involving me. While a few of them were aware that I was in seclusion working on a book, almost none of them had been told of the subject matter, so there was no good reason for this sudden interest in dreams. And yet, thanks to online services like LiveJournal, we could plainly see that from the end of November onward, over a dozen of our friends were suddenly caught up in a dream storm.

I had observed such "dream storms" in the past. I had no better word for the phenomenon. A number of people, connected through friendship or metaphysical ties, all started dreaming vividly together. Sometimes the dreams were clearly instances of dreamwalking, but more often than not, they were simply dreams that shared similar themes, as if everyone had tapped into the same stream in the collective unconscious together. The people caught up in a dream storm did not have to live in close proximity to one another. On the contrary, I was able to observe numerous instances where people were separated by hundreds of miles geographically. Several of the people caught up in a dream storm did not even know one another—but they were connected by mutual friends and they shared similar abilities and interests metaphysically. Interestingly, various people caught up in the dream storm would appear in one another's dreams. There didn't seem to be any distinct pattern to this, and on more than one occasion, a dreamer would report that so-and-so had appeared in their dreams with another person whom they did not know. The description of the unknown person closely matched someone known to the other individual who appeared in the dream but unknown to the dreamer.

I had always been fascinated by this phenomenon of shared dreams—or at least shared themes in dreams. With the advent of the Internet, and especially the prevalence of online blogs, it became easier and easier to track what people were dreaming about because they would report their dreams online. This might lead one to suspect that the shared material in the dreams arose from nothing more esoteric than the fact that everyone was reading everyone else's dream journals. Certainly there was some sharing of dreams going on between friends, but there were even more instances where two people who did not directly know one another made entries at the same time that nevertheless reflected some shared nature to their dreams. Many such journal entries were locked, so in at least a few cases, I was the only person who knew both individuals and had access to the records of their dreams. To keep things objective, I made no comments or entries myself concerning these things.

I had often wondered what triggered such dream storms. I know it might seem cliché, but one of the first times I noticed a rash of vivid, shared dreaming was in the weeks leading up to September 11, 2001. That dream storm shared themes of death, destruction, and disaster and a sense of foreboding so intense that it drove us to connect with one another and relate the dreams. For years I saved a panicked message left by a friend on my answering machine concerning a dream of terrible destruction she had just had. The message was time and date stamped 10 P.M. September 10. Another dream storm preceded the South Asian tsunami, and a third preceded the destruction of New Orleans. And yet there were countless dream storms that occurred between these massive disasters, and they were not all themed around death and destruction. Some dream storms came and went without any significant event in the outside world to indicate their nature. In the four years I had observed them, from September 11 onward, I had to admit that the ultimate pattern and meaning of dream storms was as elusive as anything that involved our dreaming minds.

The dream storm that Zamion helped track for me in November and December of 2005 was different, however. First, as near as I could tell, my own work on dreaming had inspired this rash of dreams. There was no other trigger I could identify. The themes that connected the dreams seemed to corroborate this. People dreamed of learning, of being instructed, of metaphysical experiences, of rediscovering wisdom from the past. I myself was a central figure in many of these dreams, sometimes appearing just in passing, sometimes playing the role of teacher and instructor.

I considered the possibility that I was dreamwalking to all of these people. And yet, that theory did not resonate with my own experiences. Certainly I myself was caught in the dream storm, dreaming vividly day after day. Many of my dreams were centered around the themes of metaphysical discovery and instruction that seemed to typify many of the other people's dreams, and yet most of the discoveries were unique to me. On occasion, I had a group dream, where it seemed a dozen or more of my friends were gathered together, talking about their metaphysical experiences. But these dreams were in the minority and seemed more like impromptu meetings called in the dreamtime to discuss the rest of the rash of dreams.

As I struggled to understand what was going on, my mind kept taking me back to a chart I had seen in a book on consciousness from the 1970s. The chart, put together by John Curtis Gowan for the Creating Education Foundation, was an attempt to demonstrate how telepathy worked between people, and it was based on the notion of the collective unconscious. It looked like two mountain peaks connected by a plain. The mountains represented individual consciousnesses—people, in other words. But both mountains arose from the same underlying thing, and there was no break in this foundation from mountain to mountain. This underlying plain was labeled "the collective unconscious" in the chart, and arrows indicated how the unconscious mind of the individual was connected to this larger psychic structure, and how, just as the individual fed material into the collective unconscious, the collective unconscious could pass material to the individual. As far as telepathy was concerned, the chart showed that thoughts could pass unconsciously from one person to the next via this underlying plain of connected consciousness.

The overriding idea conveyed by the chart is that our identity as completely separate individuals is illusory. On a very deep level, we have a shared psychic space. Carl Jung identified this shared psychic territory best when he developed the notion of the collective unconscious. The realm of archetypal images, universal myths and dreams, and the collective unconscious is something that we all tap into on a very deep level. It exists at a level beneath language, and it exists at a level beneath conscious awareness. Nevertheless, it is there, connecting us and very possibly providing the means for us to connect consciously with one another.

It is my opinion that this underlying connection is at work in phenomena like dream storms. If the collective unconscious can be related to the sea, and our individual minds are vessels that traverse that sea, then things like dream storms are currents that flow within that sea, currents that the little boats of our minds can get caught up in and possibly swept away by.

Unlike boats on a vast ocean, however, our "little" minds are not powerless. We seem to be able to put material into the collective unconscious just as we take material out of it. Reversing the flow may be difficult, but it can be done, as indicated by the evolution of archetypes and mythic images over time. Consider, for example, the archetype of the vampire. In the seventeenth and eighteenth centuries, vampires were the restless dead, risen corpses that preyed upon the living. When the myth of the vampire was retold in nineteenth century literature, however, it underwent a change. The vampire retained its connection to the grave and to death, but complex issues of forbidden sexuality and other out-of-bounds behaviors got added into the mix. As the archetype inspired stories, the stories fed back into the archetype, adding new layers to an already complex façade.

By the late twentieth century, the vampire archetype had inspired countless new tales in fiction and film, and the archetype evolved even further, becoming something romantic and fiercely sexual. Now, the archetype inspires an entire subculture, and the mythmaking of that subculture is again helping to change the archetype, constructing another new façade upon the framework of old connotations.

Perhaps the image of a great sea is misleading. Perhaps instead we should see the collective unconscious as an internet that connects the individual computers of our minds. Telepathy suggests that it is possible for us to send information to one another through this psychic "internet." Could it be possible for us to also hack into the system, assuming we knew enough about that system to hack it? Can a skilled individual send a mass e-mail out in the form of dreams? What about setting up chat rooms, message boards, all the online communities that make the Internet such an amazing place for endless exchange?

While I may have my theories, I don't yet have definite answers. All I can say with certainty is that dream storms happen and they seem to have some kind of significance. If we could harness such a phenomenon and participate in it consciously, we would certainly learn a great deal about ourselves, the nature of consciousness, and the experience of dreams. I am going to continue observing and gathering information on the phenomenon. I encourage you, my readers, to do the same.

APPENDIX III

SPELLS FOR DREAMING

Dream incubation was one of the primary methods for contacting spirits and gods in the ancient world. Practitioners sought spirits in dreams to reveal future events, offer insight into the feelings of a potential lover, or give a response to a personal request or prayer. In ancient Greece, one of the most common methods of dream incubation involved slaughtering a ram and offering it up as a sacrifice to the spirit or god in question. The seeker then would lay out the fleece of the ram and go to sleep. As the seeker slept in a sacred space, upon the skin of the sacrificial victim, the Gates of Dream would open to the gates of other realms, allowing gods, daimons, and even spirits of the dead access to the sleeper's dreams.

This was not the only method of dream incubation practiced in the ancient world, however. Hellenic Egypt has left us ample magickal texts outlining a variety of techniques for achieving revelatory dreams. Some of these are about as practical to attempt in this modern era as sleeping on the fleece of a ram you've just killed yourself. One spell instructs the magickal worker to acquire a human skull. The skull is treated with a number of magickal substances and fumed with incense. Although it is not overtly stated in the text, it is very probable that the skull was also decorated. Most commonly, skulls of this nature were made to look more alive, and cowry shells or gems were fixed into the sockets of their eyes. All of this attention to the skull was an attempt to make it into a kind of spirit vessel, and it was believed that the spirit that had resided in the head during life was drawn back to live there once more in death.

Once it was properly prepared, the divinatory head was set up in a special niche near the magickal worker's bed. Questions were put to the head in a ritual fashion. Sometimes the magickal worker whispered the questions into the head's ear. Sometimes they were spoken directly into the head's own mouth. Variations on this method involved writing questions out on slips of linen or papyrus and placing these in the mouth of the enchanted head. It was then believed that the spirit inhabiting the head would speak to the magickal worker in dreams, answering all the questions that had been put to it. Variations on this divinatory head can be found in a number of cultures, from Celtic Ireland to the ancient settlement of Nevali Çori.

DREAM INCUBATION

We can hardly go digging up human skulls and keeping them on our nightstands just so spirits will appear in our dreams. However, several texts have come down to us from the ancient world that contain spells that can be translated into a modern context. One of these is the *Leyden Papyrus*, a collection of spells from about the third century of the common era. From Egypt, it is written in demotic and shows the influence of a variety of religious and magickal traditions, from Alexandrian Judaism to the pantheons of ancient Greece. The *Leyden Papyrus*, torn in two parts, contains mostly spells on divination, healing, and love magick, but there is at least one spell that offers instructions on a method of dream incubation.

The following spell is in the style of a lamp inquiry and drawn from the text of "Column VI" of the *Leyden Papyrus*. The magickal text instructs the querent to gather new, unused equipment for the spell to be most effective. This is where the notion of using "virgin" items comes from. The idea is to have ritual tools that are free of any unwanted energies. New items are easiest because they have never been charged with any kind of energy. Previously used items should be thoroughly cleansed, either by grounding them energetically or cleansing them with salt.

Things you will need for this spell:
- An oil lamp
- Lamp oil, preferably natural (olive oil will do)
- A clean, new wick
- A small table
- A new brick or garden stone
- Some fresh, clean sand
- Myrrh and frankincense, preferably whole
- A quill, stylus, or old-fashioned nibbed pen
- A charcoal incense burner
- A yoga mat or futon mattress (optional)

Glass oil lamps are sold at a variety of stores, from Target to World Market. They are usually sold along with scented oils, but many of these are synthetic, and in the spirit of the spell, olive oil or a high-grade vegetable oil will probably be more desirable. If you are buying the lamp new, a new wick will come with it. Try to purchase a lamp that has a white cotton wick, because the myrrh will be used to write on the wick before submersing it in the oil.

The type of lamp that is referenced in the spell is a new lamp of white clay, and if you wish to adhere to this, there are one or two Pagan sources where I've seen clay lamps sold, most recently *SacredSource.com*—although these are terracotta (red clay) lamps. While many people who reproduce spells from ancient sources like to stick as closely to the original spell as possible, I tend to take a more lenient approach. It's the spirit of the spell that is important, at least in my opinion, and here the significance of a white clay lamp is its newness and purity. A recently purchased glass oil lamp should neatly fit these criteria.

The new brick is a little more difficult to match. Back when the *Leyden Papyrus* was being penned, new bricks were made daily, formed of straw, river clay, and sometimes animal dung, and baked in the hot Egyptian sun. We employ both different methods and different materials for bricks these days, and most comparable things you will be able to buy will be made of composite stone or concrete. Although there is certainly magickal significance connected with a newly fashioned brick of Nile mud, the more practical reason for including a brick in this spell is to have something relatively fireproof to set the oil lamp upon. If you travel down to your local hardware store and go to the lawn and garden section, you will find a variety of garden and edging stones that will serve your purposes nicely.

Frankincense, myrrh, and sand can all be purchased at a magickal shop that stocks basic incense supplies. Self-lighting charcoals should be available there as well. You will also want to consider picking up a small mortar and pestle if you don't already own one, as you will need this to crush the myrrh later. You may be able to find a quill pen or old-fashioned nibbed pen at the magickal shop as well, since these are frequently used in place of modern pens for writing a variety of spells and sigils.

Once you have all of your supplies, select a room in your house that has a convenient corner or niche that is oriented toward the south. The niche is supposed to be in a dark place, purified and clean. This arises from a tradition dating back to the nineteenth dynasty where such directionally-oriented niches were used to store ritual tools. The spell also calls for you to purify the niche with natron water. Natron is a chemical used in mummification that can only be found in its natural form in Egypt itself. A substitute form of natron can be made inexpensively at home, and I will explain the method for this after outlining the rest of the spell. If you don't want to go through the effort of making homemade natron, you can fume the corner with incense, smudge it with sage, or sprinkle it with water that has a little salt added instead. Traditionally, all of the ritual items and tools that are used in the spell would be purified prior to use as well.

You will only want the yoga mat or futon mattress if the ideal room turns out not to be your bedroom. The spell calls for you to lay out a mat in front of the lamp and sleep there, although if your bed is reasonably close to the table with the lamp, you might be able to make do.

Once you have purified the corner, purified the tools, and set the table up, grind the myrrh into powder and add a little water in order to made ink. Dip the quill or nibbed pen into this mixture and write the name *Bakhukhsikhukh* upon the wick. Place the wick in the oil lamp and pour in a quantity of oil. Place the brick upon the table and spread some sand across the brick. Place the oil lamp on top of the sand. Kneel or sit comfortably in front of the table. Light the lamp and burn frankincense in front of the lamp so the smoke curls up past the flame.

As you burn the incense, stare into the flame. Recite the name upon the wick seven times, using it like a mantra to help propel you into a trance. As you recite the name, think about what you seek to dream of. For best results, try focusing on a specific question that will be answered for you in dreams.

If you don't feel that you have sufficiently entered a trance state, place more frankincense upon the charcoal and recite the name seven more times. Repeat the mantra in sets of seven until you feel your perceptions begin to expand and your body begin to tingle or buzz. All this while, you should be peering into the flame, looking for images (another method of lamp divination involves scrying into the smoke and flames). Once the flame begins to dance with images, you have achieved the proper state of mind. By the understanding of the spell's original author, you have successfully completed a spirit-gathering, calling a spirit who will then visit you in your sleep.

At this point, the spell suggests using the following invocation:

Ho! I am Murai, Muribi, Babel, Baoth, Bamui,
The first servant of the great god,
He who giveth light exceedingly,
The companion of the flame,
He in whose mouth is the fire that is not quenched,
The great god who is seated in flames,
He who is in the midst of the fire which is in the lake of heaven,
In whose hand is the greatness and power of the gods.
Reveal thyself to me here tonight!
I pray thee to reveal thyself here to me tonight!
Speak with me and give me answer in truth and without falsehood.

A much shorter, alternative invocation appears at the end of the spell. This one omits the barbaric names and runs like this:

I pray thee to reveal thyself to me here tonight!
Speak with me and give me answer truly
Concerning the matter which I ask thee about.

After speaking the invocation out loud to the lamp, you are instructed not to speak to any other living soul for the rest of the night. With the lamp still burning, lie down in silence and go to sleep. According to the formula, the answers which you seek will come to you in dreams.

MAKING NATRON

Purists who wish to reproduce the demotic spell with as much authenticity as possible can create their own natron at home. A very good friend, Shepsumuti, gave me this easy recipe for natron. Take equal measures of sea salt and baking soda. Add a small amount of water and mix them into a thick paste. Spread the paste onto a cookie sheet and bake it in an oven at about 150 degrees Fahrenheit for fifteen to twenty minutes, or until it dries out completely. It should look like a slightly cracked slab of chalk.

Take the mixture out of the oven and allow it to cool, then break it up into smaller pieces. Store these pieces in airtight containers until you require them for use. A small amount of natron will dissolve completely in water. Water treated this way is considered ritually pure in most Egyptian traditions—essentially, it's Egyptian holy water. This ritually pure water is not only used in the previous spell, but it is also a prime component of most Kemetic spellwork.

PILLOW CHARMS

Another ancient form of dreamwork can be found in the folk traditions handed down to us by our European ancestors. Most of these are spells for divining the name of one's true love. There are many variations on this spell, but many of them ultimately instruct the querent to place something under his or her pillow. A vision of the future love would manifest in dreams, or the future lover's name would be whispered in dreams. Sometimes the item was placed not under the pillow but under the bed itself. Either way, the key to this magickal endeavor involved incubating upon an item that resonated with the desired question.

As far as magick goes, spells like this function on the notion that like attracts like. If you sleep on something invested with a particular sort of energy, that item will draw that energy into your dreams or, ultimately, into your life. From a psychological perspective, the practice also makes sense. By taking the time to craft a charm or write out a specific request, you are essentially programming your subconscious to focus on this. The act of placing the item under your pillow or under your bed is further invested with symbolism, and the act primes your subconscious to associate the question or item with sleep and dreams. In many ways, the activity of placing a charm under your pillow in order to invoke a specific dream is simply a more concrete version of repeating what you want to dream about before you fall asleep. Either way, you have put in a call to your subconscious, requesting that it give some attention to the item in question. Inevitably, that attention will manifest in dreams.

Modern dreamworkers can certainly make use of these archaic techniques. Everyone has different approaches that work best, but the way we discover our best methods is through experimenting with a variety of techniques. If it is your goal to dreamwalk to a specific person, try reciting that person's name before you fall asleep. If that doesn't seem to be working for you, try falling back on folk wisdom.

Make a charm that represents the person in question and place this under your pillow at night. Write the person's name out on a fancy piece of paper and slip this into your pillow case. If you truly want to capture the feel of folk magick with this exercise, you'll want to write the name out three times. Seven and nine are also powerful numbers, so if three does not seem enough to you, write the name seven times or nine times on the same slip of paper, then keep this charm under your pillow at night. Before you go to sleep, take the charm out and recite the name as many times as you have it written out. Close your eyes and focus on the person, then place the charm back under your pillow and go to sleep. The more you invest the activity with meaning and intent, the more powerfully it will appeal to your subconscious, so make a ritual out of it each night. You might even consider lighting some incense and fuming the room before sleeping in order to create or more magickal mood.

DREAM SHRINES

Several of my friends have created little shrines to the people that they share strong connections with. These shrines have photos of the people in question as well as items associated with each individual. Names are written out in fancy calligraphy and placed under the photos or among the items that represent each person. A shrine like this can be kept near your bed and you can contemplate it before going to sleep each night. Making this a ritual you observe each night will help to solidify the bonds between you and these other people, and reaching out along those bonds before falling asleep can help insure that you will reach out to these people first when dreamwalking.

Recite the names of these people who are the closest and most important connections you maintain in this life. If you have items belonging to the people, pick these up and handle them. Feel the energy of each individual lingering on their tokens. Use these things to reach out and close the distance between you so that when you sleep, you naturally reach out to them in dreams. If there is one person in particular from the group that you wish to focus on in dreams, take that person's token and place it under your pillow while you sleep. Consider rotating whose item you place beneath your pillow so that you give special attention to a different individual each night.

An even more potent variation of this dream shrine is to have all the people who appear in your shrine also keep shrines of their own, each with a token and a photo that represents you. Think of these as magickal beacons that each of you light up before you go to sleep, guiding one another through the realm of dreams.

BIBLIOGRAPHY

Barber, Paul. *Vampires, Burial, and Death*. Yale University Press, New Haven, CT: 1988

Brennan, J.H. *The Astral Projection Workbook*. Sterling Publishing Co., New York, NY: 1990

Buhlman, William. *Adventures Beyond the Body*. HarperSanFrancisco, San Francisco, CA: 1996

Cave, Janet. *Dreams and Dreaming*. Time-Life Books, Alexandria, VA: 1990

Denning, Melita and Osborne Phillips. *Astral Projection*. Llewellyn Publications, St. Paul, MN: 1994

Eliade, Mircea. *Shamanism: Archaic Techniques of Ecstasy*. Bollingen Series. Princeton University Press, Princeton, NJ: 1964

Fortune, Dion. *Applied Magic*. The Aquarian Press, Northhamptonshire, England: 1987

Fortune, Dion. *Aspects of Occultism*. Samuel Weiser, Inc., New York, NY: 1979

Fortune, Dion. *Psychic Self-Defense*. Weiser Books, Boston, MA: 2001

George, Leonard. *Alternative Realities: the Paranormal, the Mystic, and the Transcendent in Human Experience*. Facts on File, New York, NY: 1995

Gowan, John Curtis. *Trance, Art, and Creativity*. Creating Education Foundation, Buffalo, NY: 1975

Griffith, F. and Herbert Thompson, *The Leyden Papyrus*. Dover Books Inc., New York, NY: 1974

Harner, Michael. *The Way of the Shaman*. Tenth anniversary edition. HarperSan Francisco, San Francisco, CA: 1990

Hufford, David J. *The Terror that Comes in the Night*. University of Pennsylvania Press, Philadelphia, PA: 1982

Konstantinos. *Vampires: the Occult Truth*. Llewellyn Publications, St. Paul, MN: 1996

Lang, Andrew. *The Book of Dreams and Ghosts*. Causeway Books, New York, NY: 1974

McMoneagle, Joseph. *Remote Viewing Secrets*. Hampton Roads Publishing, Charlottesville, VA: 2000

Monroe, Robert A. *Journeys Out of the Body*. Broadway Books, New York, NY: 1977

Muldoon, Sylvan and Hereward Carrington. *The Projection of the Astral Body*. Weiser Books, Boston, MA: 1973

Ogden, Daniel. *Greek and Roman Necromancy*. Princeton University Press, Princeton, NJ: 2001

Perls, Fritz. *The Gestalt Approach & Eye Witness to Therapy*. Science and Behavior Books, New York, NY: 1973

Rheingold, Howard. *They Have a Word for It*. Sarabande Books, Louisville, KY: 1988

Slate, Joe H. *Astral Projection and Psychic Empowerment*. Llewellyn Publications, St. Paul, MN: 1998

Thurman, Robert A. F. *The Tibetan Book of the Dead*. Quality Paperback Book Club, New York, NY: 1998

Ullman, Montague and Stanley Krippner. *Dream Telepathy*. Macmillan Publishing Co., New York, NY: 1973

Van de Castle, Robert. *Our Dreaming Mind*. Ballantine Books, New York, NY: 1994